PAUL'S LETTER to the CORINTHIANS 55 A.D.

Sanford G. Shetler

Christian Light Publications, Inc.
Harrisonburg, Virginia 22801

FOREWORD

This "Compact Commentary" on Paul's First Letter to the Corinthians comes out of some years of private study in the Pauline Epistles and marks the beginning of what we hope may become in time a series of studies on the epistles.

There is a new movement under way which is encouraging. I refer to the rise of Bible study and "koinonia" groups in various circles across the land among young and old. Some have hinted at the possibility of a new Reformation, as people, disillusioned with many misleading philosophies and theologies, once more turn to the Bible itself for *answers*. It is this kind of resurgence of interest that has helped make Dr. Francis Schaeffer's experiment at L'Abri Fellowship in Switzerland such a great success. Young intellectuals from all over the world, despairing of the existential dilemma, are literally beating a path to his door to discover for the first time the living relevance of the plain and simple truths of the Bible. In his book, *Escape from Reason,* Schaeffer notes that while some churchmen in recent years have said repeatedly that "God-talk" no longer communicates, quite to the contrary "it is possible to take the system the Bible teaches to the market place and let it stand there and speak for itself."

It is the candid belief of this author that the Bible is to a large extent its own best interpreter. Comparing Scripture with Scripture, noting how the passages are constructed and related to each other in the total context, often becomes the best key to interpretation. Much of this technique was learned from our good friend, the late Bishop John L. Stauffer, President of Eastern Mennonite College.

This small work is not merely an expanded paraphrase or an amalgam of versions but represents a fresh attempt to uncover the message of the Epistle. We readily acknowledge, of course, our dependence on many other helps and commentaries.

In our present study we have become impressed with the strong internal coherence of the Epistle. We do not accept the ready thesis of some commentators who over-stress the human element of authorship

iii

that Paul was not too consistent in his writing, rather disjunct in fact, jumping almost recklessly from topic to topic in cyclopedic fashion. Quite to the contrary one is impressed in a careful study of the Epistle with the logical sequence of the various passages. The divine dimensions are very evident. It is this, of course, that gives perennial and universal significance to New Testament writings. Certainly I Corinthians is not provincial—neither by time nor place.

Too many of us are far too satisfied to get our knowledge of the Scriptures second-handed from those we consider more competent. But we should never allow the church of our time to fall into the Medieval fallacy of leaving Scriptural interpretation to only the professional theologians and trained clergy. Unfortunately many intellectuals who normally place a high value on the use of primary sources in research are quite content to gain their knowledge of the Bible from secondary sources. All this would not be too bad if the secondary sources were not so frequently bad. Jesus' own statement comes to mind as an encouragement to all who want to know God's Word but who feel the lack of professional expertise. Many of the profound truths, said Christ, are hidden "from the wise and prudent and revealed to babes."

Once and again after hours of meditation and study, sometimes in the early morning hours, one arrives at that exciting moment when new light falls on a given passage and the Bible becomes alive. It is probably too true that few people will ever experience the thrill of this adventure.

The immediate inspiration for the preparation of this volume came through conducting several studies in this Epistle within the past year, the first for the youth and adults of a group of churches at Johnstown, Pennsylvania, and the second for adults at the Lindale Church near Harrisonburg, Virginia. Through these studies my earlier fascination for the Epistle as a practical handbook for the church of our time was reaffirmed. The experience also helped confirm my opinion, derived after many years of teaching children, youth, and adults, that there is no need for sugar-coating of the Word of God to make it palatable. The conventional style of writing in this book is

iv

based on this very premise.

The format of this "Compact Commentary" is somewhat unique. You will note that the numbers of the verses appear in the margin leaving the text more readable. It has also been written in a style that makes it possible to read the commentary as a book without the use of the Bible itself. Verses appearing in parentheses are cross references to help clarify the meaning.

Because many people still prefer and use the classical King James translation, this commentary is based on that version. Careful comparisons have been made, however, with numerous other versions, and also, of course, with the original Greek text. In some instances we have disregarded the "accepted" interpretation of a given passage for what we considered a more appropriate rendering on the basis of "internal evidence."

A special feature is the topical index with many of the topics listed in current lingo. Does Paul, for example, speak on "Social Action," or "Situational Ethics," or "Racial Equality"? Such topics as these are listed with the verses and sections of the letter which deal with them.

Criticism may be levelled at the author for the lengthy treatment given the first part of chapter 11 which deals with the women's veiling. It is an attempt to make up for some of the current lack of serious expositions on this section of Paul's letter. It is his belief that this section cannot be lightly passed off as irrelevant for our time. It is not that we consider this specific teaching as of greater importance than any other section of the Epistle.

It is our prayer that as you use this book, you may receive new confidence in the Word of God as the Word of God. We also pray that the same Holy Spirit who authored the Epistle through Paul will cause you to abound in "wisdom and grace, and understanding," that you may become fruitful saints in the church of the living Christ!

Sanford G. Shetler
Eastern Mennonite College
1971

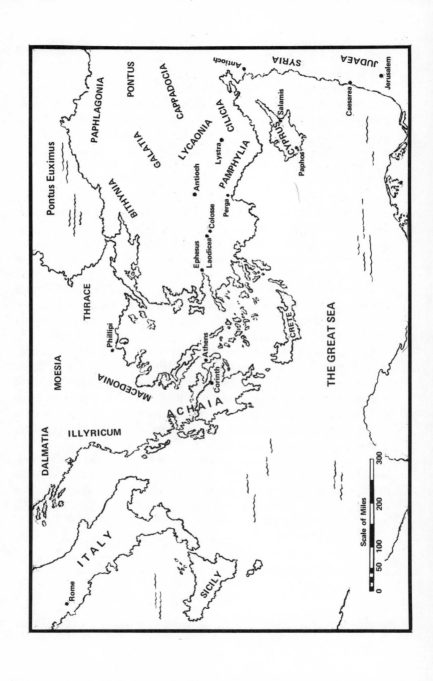

CONTENTS

APPROACH

How we approach the Bible has much to say as to how we leave it when we lay it down again to return to the tasks of life. Is the Bible merely a kind of *"read" book* that bestows some mysterious values on the one who reads a few verses daily? Is it a *rule book* that furnishes us with a legal code to live by and to make us proper members of God's household? ... *Or* is it a *real book* that breathes a living message from God?

"The Word became flesh" suggests that it becomes effective only when it becomes a living part of us—a counterpart of the historic Incarnation. As the Living Word, it is not mystical or idealistic but realistic. It is not a fetish to be revered for its magical powers, a relic to be cherished. It is not a part of the bridal regalia or something to be placed under folded hands in a casket.

It is in every sense of the term, the Word. It is the *Way,* the *Truth,* the *Life.*

A great Bible scholar centuries ago, comparing the Bible with secular books, noted that whereas secular knowledge needed first to be understood to be appreciated, the Bible had to be appreciated first before it could be understood.

We are living in a day when the Bible is being regarded more and more as merely another book. How it came to be written, its style and authorship—all are set forth as tests of its authenticity. Parts that fail to meet all these tests are considered apocryphal, or as folklore. Ironically, however, the parts supposed to be "genuine" are given no greater hearing, in terms of being accepted authoritatively or binding, than those parts considered less authentic. The over-all effect of this is that men come to question the whole Bible. Modern theology maintains that the Bible is not a God-given revelation but merely a "record, witness, and medium of revelation." The Bible, it is claimed, contains many errors and contradictions and is therefore not infallible.

The fact though that men in this century have gone almost

"version-crazy" trying to translate the Bible into the language of the man on the street betrays the fact that it is no ordinary book. This same kind of thing is not happening to any other "classic." High schools and colleges, for example, are still using the "authorized version" of Shakespeare's plays which were written in exactly the same period as the King James version of the Bible. This does not argue necessarily for the use of that version, but it does indicate the universal judgment that the Bible is a Word all men should know.

How we approach this letter, then, makes all the difference in the world. If the "Pauline Epistles," accepted by historic Christianity as a part of the inspired "canon" (the actual set of inspired writings), were written merely by a religious leader of a tiny group of religionists of the First Century, that is one thing. If, on the other hand, these were written by one of God's chosen messengers under the inspiration of the Holy Spirit, as we believe they were, then that is something else.

The difference between Divine Revelation and human writings is more than *quantitative* in terms of representing the *"God element"*; it is *qualitative*. It is this distinguishing quality that caused the church fathers to give Paul's writings an equal place with the Law and the Prophets and with the sayings of Jesus.

One should approach the Bible with reverence and with a prayer that the Holy Spirit may open its pages in a way that will make it live in the heart.

BACKGROUND

Corinth

To understand Paul's letter to the church at Corinth it is important to know something of the city itself. One gains a new appreciation for this young church when he understands the pagan culture in which it was planted.

Corinth, second city of importance in Achaia, was a large metropolis. There were probably few Christian inhabitants although some have estimated that there may have been literally hundreds. It was a comparatively new city having been rebuilt 46 B.C. The old city destroyed by the Roman armies had lain in ashes for a century. Well situated as a shipping port, it became a crossroads for commerce and a mecca for travellers. It was furthermore a recreation center, the site of the famous Isthmian games. Stalker compares the two cities of Athens and Corinth to Scotland's leading cities—Edinburgh, the intellectual center, and Glasgow, its principal commercial center.

The city was built on a low tableland joined to the immediate south by the Acrocorinthus, a rocky citadel rising 2000 feet above the sea. From its summit, which was large enough to accommodate a city, one could see on a clear day the city of Athens 40 miles to the east. Situated on an isthmus, Corinth was known as "The City of Two Seas." At the edge of the city were three harbors which made Corinth the noted center for trade between East and West. A considerable portion of the temple of Apollo which survived the sack of Rome was already 600 years old when Paul arrived there. Seven columns nearly 25 feet high and 6 feet in diameter at the base remain today as a remnant of the once magnificent temple.

The city which Paul entered "with weakness and much fear and trembling," like Athens, was dominated with idolatry. The great temple of Aphrodite, situated 1000 feet above the level of the city on the citadel, was in constant view of the townsfolk. Connected with its worship were 1000 "consecrated prostitutes," who enriched the temple "with their sanctified vice." To live like a Corinthian or to be "Corinthianized" meant in those times living a life of luxury and licentiousness. It was often said by those familiar with its luxury and evils that travellers could not afford a visit to Corinth.

The immoral trade was carried on chiefly with shipmates and traders who visited the port. Such shameless vice struck despair into the heart of Paul, yet it was also a challenge. The wealth and vice of the city were coupled with a kind of pseudo-culture based on the "wisdom of the world" which Paul referred to so frequently in his letter. While all this militated against the simple Gospel message and the possibility of building a spiritual church, there was, however, a kind of freedom here that was not found in intellectual Athens. As a field of service, its potential was unlimited, and Paul saw this as a most strategic center to launch the Gospel. Those who received the Gospel here could carry it to the frontiers of the Empire and beyond.

Considering the moral condition of the city, its wealth and its sophistry, starting a church in such a place is alone a tribute to Paul's unusual ability as a church organizer. But it is even a greater tribute to his unshakeable faith in the power of the living Gospel to transform the lives of sinful men.

Paul

Critics have not been easy on Paul. Some have questioned his authority to write words that are given equal place with the words of Jesus. His style has been variously described as disjunct and involved. He has been accused of trying to establish a Christianity which Jesus never preached—for misinterpreting the Gospel.

Yet Paul continues to be an interesting figure in history. His world-wide impact is totally disproportionate to the scope of his contributions. Judging him by all the usual standards of greatness, it is inconceivable that a man who did no more than organize a number of churches in Turkey, Greece and Italy and then write some letters to these same churches should go down in history as a great man, or that his letters should be anything more today than collectors' items.

Few men have been studied and written about like Paul. The

library at Harvard is said to contain 2000 books on his life and letters. Novelists of our century are still writing about him.

In his day Paul was able to reach men in the top echelons of society including some in Caesar's own household. He had to be reckoned with as a force in the Empire by no less a figure than the Emperor himself. And it was, in fact, through Paul's preaching and the establishment of Christianity within the Roman Empire that its corrupt practices finally came to an end. The social ills of the day, slavery, infanticide and gross vice all fell under the impact of the Gospel he was "not ashamed to preach."

Apparently diminutive in stature and with some marked physical infirmity—some say diseased eyes, others an impediment of speech—Paul did not present an imposing figure. Yet even the rhetoric-conscious Corinthians had to admit that while his speech was "contemptible," his letters were "weighty and powerful." His preaching was "in demonstration of the power of God."

Men have tried to describe Paul as a missionary, evangelist, bishop and founder of churches. But his greatness defies description. Careful reading of his epistles reveals the inner dynamics of this great man. He was not harsh, dogmatic or unfeeling as critics have frequently charged. He was a man of tears and compassion and human understanding. At one place he refers to himself as a nurse who takes care of her patients with compassion. He struggled as most men do with the ordinary problems of making a living, and though he sometimes wanted, he had learned in "whatsoever state [he was] therewith to be content." He knew what persecution was and inner turmoil as well. His experience in Macedonia and Achaia was trying, so trying, in fact, that at one point he despaired of life. To him, the more he loved, the less he was loved. When he hazarded his life for the Gospel and was jailed, his enemies found reason to blame *him.* Some despised his preaching. He was accused for being less than truthful. Yet in all these things, whether persecution, famine, peril or sword he could write that we are "more than conquerors through him that loved us." He had a great burden for his own people, the Jews. His heart's desire was "that they might be saved." In his own life and conduct he came about the nearest to the life and character of Jesus of any man who ever lived. His unflagging zeal carried him over a wide span of territory—as far north as the Balkans, as far west as Spain, and as far south as Gaza—all in a time when travel and communication was most difficult. He literally spent himself so that the Gospel might be brought to the far-flung reaches of the Empire. He died at last a martyr for the great Cause he loved.

In 1964 it was our privilege to stand on that "sacred" spot where tradition has it that he was beheaded by Nero in the year A.D. 69. It brought to mind his farewell near the end of his life: "I have fought a good fight, I have finished my course, I have kept the faith. Henceforth there is laid up for me a crown of righteousness."

Paul in Corinth

Like the famous William Penn who spent less than two years living in the colony he founded, Paul spent less than two years with his new church at Corinth. But Paul had founded many churches and had many charges, and thus had to distribute his time and labors.

It was on his second missionary journey that his ministry first touched the city of Corinth. This particular tour has been called one of the greatest expeditions of its kind in missionary history. Stalker goes even further, comparing it with the expeditions of Alexander the Great and Julius Caesar, and rating it as "perhaps the most momentous recorded in the annals of the human race." Its scope, as indicated already, included Central and Southeast Asia Minor, Phyrgia, Galatia, and Troas, and in Europe the great centers of Philippi, Thessalonica, Berea, Athens, and Corinth.

True to his usual custom, Paul preached in the synagogue every Sabbath. He tried to bring the Gospel to his own people first. Before long, however, he met with severe opposition and so turned to the Gentiles. He was offered the use of the house of Justus, a God-fearing Gentile who lived next to the synagogue. The city's population was cosmopolitan, being composed of freedmen and slaves, pagans and Jews, descendants of the early Roman colonists and native Greeks, not to mention the constant flow of travellers and traders. Paul had unlimited possibilities.

Many turned to Christ, mostly from the Gentile population and were baptized as a result of Paul's preaching, although he baptized few himself. Among them was Crispus, a ruler of the synagogue, "and all his house." His unusual success at producing converts in such a short time still puzzles the minds of missionaries who have labored for years in a given area before realizing any "visible" results.

Among the friends that Paul made in Corinth from the beginning of his stay was Aquilla and his wife Priscilla. They with all Jews had been expelled from Rome under order of Claudius and had taken up residence here some six or seven months prior to Paul's arrival. It seems that he made his home with them for the major portion of the time he stayed here, helping them in their trade of tentmaking, a skill he had acquired no doubt as a young Hebrew lad in the good Hebrew tradition of teaching the young trades.

During Paul's stay in Corinth, Gallio, the elder brother of the famous Roman philosopher, Seneca, came to govern Achaia as proconsul. This was 51 A.D. Certain Jews, feeling the impact of Paul's ministry, brought accusation against him saying he was preaching a religion contrary to Roman law. Gallio, not particularly concerned about religious matters, refused to admit the case for trial and dismissed them. Following this the Greek bystanders, venting their feelings against the Jews, beat Sosthenes, the chief ruler of the synagogue, Gallio standing by without interfering. His casual attitude in the matter had the effect of an authoritative decision that Paul's preaching was not an offense against Roman law.

Little is known of the subsequent history of the Corinthian church and the exact details of the respective ministries of those who labored there. Bible scholars differ on the exact number of visits Paul himself made and the number of letters he wrote. Morris, by comparing the various Scriptures, believes he made altogether three visits and wrote four letters, two of which have been lost. Among those who labored here in addition to those mentioned, were Timothy, Silas, and Apollos.

Paul apparently paid a brief visit to Corinth on his third missionary journey, although some hold he did this later from Macedonia. While at Ephesus he wrote a letter which has not been preserved. A reply to this plus an oral report of some of their problems led to the writing of I Corinthians. This was probably sent by Titus. At least it was sent to Corinth about this time.

Ruins of Ancient Corinth, Greece

Photo by H. Armstrong Roberts

Photo by J. Otis Yoder

Acrocorinthus

Photo by J. Otis Yoder

Shop and Temple of Apollos

For God, who commanded the light to shine out of darkness, hath shined in our hearts, to give the light of the knowledge of the glory of God in the face of Jesus Christ.

—II Corinthians 4:6

The Bible was never intended to be a book for scholars and specialists only. From the beginning it was intended to be everybody's book, and that is what it continues to be like. The message which it contains is designed to meet a universal need; its central figure is rightly called "the Saviour of the World." Although it was completed such a long time ago, the Bible never grows out of date, because the subjects with which it deals are those subjects which retain their relevance from one century to another, and concern us today as vitally as they concerned the people who first read the Bible.

F. F. Bruce, Rylands Professor of Biblical Criticism and Exegesis, University of Manchester (England)

CHAPTER I

SAINTS–IN–THE–MAKING   LEADER CULTS
PREACHING OF THE CROSS
WORLDLY WISDOM VERSUS THE WISDOM OF GOD

Called as an Apostle (1)

Paul opens his noteworthy letter to the Christian **1**
"assembly" at Corinth in the typical style of the day, his
own name first, and states at once his official position
under the authority of Christ. That he in no way
attempted, however, to establish any kind of ecclesias-
tical hierarchy is seen in the humble way in which he
includes Sosthenes his "brother" in his salutation. This
was to be a new brotherhood of believers unlike that of
any other religion, and there was to be no "sacred" class
of clergy and "common" laity. Who this Sosthenes was
or what part he may have had in writing this letter is not
clear, but it is likely that this was the same Sosthenes
mentioned in Acts 18, a converted Jew of Corinth who
had once been the ruler of the synagogue. He had been
beaten at one time by some of the Greek citizens of
Corinth and was therefore dear to Paul as a fellow-
laborer in suffering.

The high value Paul placed on his personal call always
comes through clearly in all his letters. There was never
any doubt in his own mind as to who he was or what his
place was in God's program. The office of the apostle
was unique. It was a special office for a chosen group at
the beginning of the Christian era. It was at the head of   **(12:29)**

5

the list of offices mentioned later in the letter. Paul had not been an eyewitness of Christ from the baptism of John until He was taken into heaven, which apparently was the qualifying mark of an apostle when Matthias was selected to fill the vacancy created by the death of Judas. As "one born out of due time," Paul had met Christ on the road to Damascus at the time of his conversion. The apostles were the original "sent ones" to launch the Christian witness of the Gospel.

(Acts 1:22)

(I Cor. 15:8)

(Acts 9)

Called as Saints (2-3)

2   While few were called as apostles, who would want to conjecture how many have been called as saints? Even the *sent ones* had first to become the *saved ones*. It is man's highest ambition to hold high positions in the world, but there is no higher calling than sainthood. And whatever our earthly vocation, it must ever become secondary to the heavenly calling.

Paul's view of the church was no less clear than his view of his own role as an apostle. It was not *his* church—it was the "assembly" of God. He saw the church, too, as being made up of individual members and makes frequent reference to particular persons. "Sanctified" means set apart for a special purpose. The church is not an integral part of the world. Paul recognized the local character of the church. It is not something nebulous. It is represented in specific groups at specific places. But at the same time Paul's view of the universal nature of the church is also apparent. Someone has referred to the "sweet catholicity" of Paul, which allowed him to include in his thinking "all who in every place call upon the name of Jesus Christ." But this very expression of *inclusiveness* also underscores the *exclusiveness* of the Gospel. It is only in *Christ* that man can find true unity. True ecumenicity in the modern context

6

would include all who *truly* call upon Jesus as Lord and would in no case suggest conglomerate unions of denominations in which much of the leadership has long since rejected Jesus as the supernaturally-born Son of God.

For Paul to speak of the "saints" at Corinth is rather interesting in light of their many problems and their carnality. Someone has said that every good pastor sees before him two congregations: one, as it is, with all of its faults and imperfections—"saints-in-the-making," the other, the church as he hopes it to be. In this kind of "bifocal" view Paul could easily write, "I thank my God always on your behalf . . ." His greeting, which is in the form of a blessing pronounced upon them, shows the warmth he held for the churches he founded. Comparing this with his later reprimand for their arrogance and carnality, one finds that Paul also saw before him two congregations.

3, 4

Paul's Prayer (4-9)

Paul's prayer here, as his other pastoral prayers in the various epistles, is a study in itself, a model, in fact, for other pastors. It reflects his love and concern and gives us a clue as to why his first letter to the Corinthians proved so effective. One may call I Corinthians a letter of discipline, but it was bathed in prayer. His whole prayer represents his thankfulness for their *present state,* midst their imperfections and carnality, recognizing the faltering light of their "smoking flax" which he did not wish to quench. He prayed earnestly that they would remain faithful to the end. There is much emotion packed into this large-hearted prayer. Hear him pray:

5

(See II Cor. 2:7)

(Matt. 12:20)

I thank God for the grace of God given you by
    Jesus Christ:
      — that in everything ye are enriched by him

4

5

7

	— in all utterance (ability to say what you know)
	— in all knowledge (ability to know)
6	— that the testimony of Christ was confirmed in you, and
7 (Ch. 12)	— that ye come behind in no gift
	— [you are] waiting for the coming of our Lord Jesus Christ
8	— who shall confirm you unto the end—blameless
9	— who (as a faithful God to see you through) called you into the fellowship *(koinonia)* of his Son.

Some significant concerns emerge in this prayer. In some sense he is presupposing qualities in their life (and thanking God for them) which they needed to possess. Was he, for instance, alluding to their eagerness to speak in tongues when he spoke of their being enriched "in all utterance," and that they "came behind in no gift"? Does the order here, utterance before knowledge, indicate that they spoke sometimes before they had knowledge? From subsequent statements it appears, in fact, that their knowledge was sometimes ignorance and their utterances unintelligible prattle.

(Chs. 12, 14)

The idea of *koinonia* (fellowship) is uniquely Christian, representing a closely knit, interacting body of like-minded believers. This was a fitting prelude to Paul's remarks in the next few paragraphs on their divisiveness.

The prayer, in short, almost overreaches what Paul actually saw in his people, and as indicated before, might well be a model prayer for pastors who may have a tendency to be short-visioned or easily disheartened.

It is significant too that Paul makes such frequent reference to Christ. The person and power of Christ was central in his preaching and ministry. In the thirty-one verses of this chapter the name of Christ is mentioned no less than eighteen times (once by pronoun and once in the name "Lord"). In the first ten verses Christ is mentioned in every verse. Note the various combinations which cover the whole relationship of Christ to the believer:

1. called of Christ
2. sanctified in Christ
3. peace through Christ
4. grace from Christ
5. enriched by Christ
6. confirmed in Christ   **1-10**
7. waiting for the coming of Christ
8. blameless through Christ
9. fellowship in Christ
10. unity in Christ

The Divisions (10-16)

Paul affectionately "beseeches" (appeals to) them to be united *in thought and judgment,* which is obviously the basis of all unity. A very apparent reason for writing   **10** to the Corinthians in the first place was their lack of unity, reported to them by the family of Chloe. There   **11** was something very earthy about the early Christians at Corinth. Although this deserved rebuke, it seems to move us so close to them. The homey, chatty approach, which brings us down rapidly from the mountain-top experience of sainthood to the valley of day-by-day living, also moves us rapidly across the centuries to the life of a church which was much like ours today.

They were split into factions over leaders. Some were   **12** for Paul, some for Apollos, and still others for Cephas. There is some evidence, according to commentators, that Cephas (Peter) had once visited here, apparently long enough for some of the members at Corinth to have become "Cephas men." Little is known of Apollos, but from the Book of Acts we do gain some interesting

(Acts 18: 24-28)

information. He was a very eloquent speaker, mighty in the Scripture and fervent in spirit. Whether his name itself is significant is not clear, but his qualities are somewhat symbolized in the characteristics attributed to the Greek god, Apollo, the god of sunlight, prophecy, music, and poetry. He seemed to be all of that. A converted Jew himself, with his knowledge of the Law and through his eloquent preaching, he "mightily convinced the Jews, and that, publicly, showing by the Scriptures that Jesus was Christ." That he was not at first fully grounded in the new faith, however, is shown by the fact that Paul's new found friends and fellow-laborers in tent-making, Aquilla and his wife Priscilla, took him aside and expounded "unto him the way of God more perfectly." He was, in short, capable and dynamic, and ready to learn, but at the same time the kind of leader who could easily surround himself with "fans" without even trying. Paul, in later references to him, recognizes

(3:6; 16:12)

his contribution to the church. He did not consider him a rival.

But there was still another group at Corinth, a group which professed to be above the leader cults. They claimed none of these men, Paul, Cephas, or Apollos, as

12

their champion, but insisted that they were simply for *Christ*. But their arrogance was no less manifest, for in essence they were giving *no* recognition to the ministers who had labored so earnestly for them.

13

The whole situation represented juvenile conduct and was ridiculous and hurtful, yet they probably did not see it in this light. If they were divided, it was certain that Christ was not divided, and yet they claimed to belong to Christ! Paul, important as he was, had after all not been the one who was crucified for them, and he very

14-16

judiciously avoided baptizing many converts lest he would have a following of persons who could claim special honors at some later time for having been baptized by *Paul!*

This party spirit, although considered a sign of "democracy at work" in the frame of modern democratic governments or even within the Greek body politic, has never been part of the mode of operation for the Christian church. Each minister has his own gifts and place, and there is no need ever for competition. Paul returns to this thought again in chapter 4 where he **(4:6)** speaks again of himself and Apollos.

"The Gospel" and Worldly Wisdom (17-31)

An analysis of Paul's writings reveals his deep love for **17** the "Gospel." To him it was an endearing term which he used very frequently. It was his life, love, and message. It was also his method. He wrote:

> For Christ sent me not to baptize, but to *preach the* **17, 18** *Gospel (evaggelizesthai):* not with wisdom of *words (logos),* lest the cross of Christ should be of none effect. For the *preaching (logos)* of the cross is to them that perish foolishness (absurdity), but unto us which are saved it is the power of God.

The Greeks were well familiar with the term *sophia* **19-21** (wisdom or philosophy) but it took Christianity to introduce the words *evangelize* and *preach,* which meant "to announce" or "to proclaim" the "glad tidings." It is also clear from Pauline theology that there are two classes of people, "them that perish" and "us which are saved."

While to the worldly wise preaching was foolishness, since it lacked the intrigue of logic and rhetoric, to Paul, who saw the value of it in changing mankind, it was "the power of God." For intriguing as the high-sounding philosophies may be, they can never change men's lives. At the heart of the Gospel is the Cross. Paul never moved away from this very far in his preaching. As a "sent one" he had been called to proclaim the Good News as a message grounded in the historical fact of the crucifixion (and resurrection). There was no "myth" in Paul's theology, and the "I-Thou" relationship, between Man and God, which he preached could only be achieved through the Cross.

He contrasts the *preaching of the Cross* with the *wisdom of this world.* Philosophers, thinkers, writers, debaters, had their systems of logic, but they were not impressive. Note the use of the terms which described the kind of wisdom this represented:

17   "wisdom of words (word)" — their rhetoric, logic, and eloquence

19   "wisdom of the wise" — the intellectualism of the sophists

20   "wisdom of the world" — the philosophy of the cosmos—naturalism, rationalism.

20   Worldly wisdom is simply foolishness with God, and

(II Tim. 3:7) through it the world will never come to know God or Truth, even though they will be "ever learning"—"The

21   world by wisdom knew not God." The Jehovah-oriented

22   Jews were always looking for God-manifestations (signs) —*God reaching down* to prove Himself—but the philosophically-minded Greeks were always *reaching up* with their human wisdom in search of the highest good, to prove themselves. Paul was keenly aware of the two classes in his audience. In sharp contrast Paul was

23   preaching Christ crucified. The perfect participial form of the verb *crucified* denotes a continuing process which must be constantly reenacted in the life of the believer. What man needs is not *signs* or *philosophy* but the *Gospel.* Signs, representing the spectacular, appeal to the emotions, while philosophy, representing the rational, appeals to the intellect. But the Gospel, minimizing both of these, presents a Person, Christ, and His finished

12

work of redemption through the cross.

The cross ever remained a stumbling block to the Jews and "absurdity" to the Greeks. It was a stumbling **23** block to the Jews since it represented a dishonorable form of death and at the same time a complete denial of the kind of Messiah they were anticipating. To the Greeks who trusted in complex systems of thought, it was too simple. Yet to the *believing Jews and Greeks* Christ became the *power* (miracle-working power) and **24** the *wisdom* of the omnipotent and omnisicient God. **(See Matt. 28:18)**

Thus what was regarded as foolishness by Greek Sophists (lovers of wisdom), was always seen by the Christians in its true light as logical and sound. Wonderful as the Greeks were in their achievements—and they must be honored for their many contributions— their philosophies offered no satisfying solution to man's **25** present or future needs. God at His weakest—if one can conceive this thought—is infinitely stronger than man at his best.

This is still true today. There are philosophers and philosophic theologians who profess to "speak to this age," but only those who proclaim the glad tidings can really speak to *men*. And while science and learning have lifted many of man's physical burdens, man's inventions have outstripped his power to control them. And certainly when men face the greatest tragedies and stresses of life, including death itself, it is not the scientist or the philosopher to whom they turn for consolation and help, but to those who have the Eternal Wisdom in their hearts.

Because the divine proclamation is in their minds too **26-28** simple, not many wise men and not many important men will become Christians. It is, in fact, through the foolish *things* of the world—those things which appear foolish to the worldly wise—that the wise are confounded. And it is through those who are regarded weak, and through the "low-born" ("base-things"—KJV) that God works. An interesting idea is suggested here which relates to verse 25. Might Paul be saying that God's extension of Himself is man—and it is through this weakest part of God, when dedicated to Him, that He performs His work?

Paul lays much emphasis on the words "wisdom" and "power," the two terms that apply to man's chief goals and ambitions. Man, with all of his strength and wisdom, is, in God's sight *nothing,* for it is not on this basis that God's approval is gained. Else it would be a matter of **29** competition in which the wisest and most accomplished would win and those of low esteem and of little accomplishment would be lost. It is Christ who is our **30** *wisdom,* our *righteousness,* our *sanctification* and *redemption.* These latter terms, unknown to the Greeks, represent God's supernatural work upon the heart of man. So, then, if there is any boasting to be done, let it be in the Lord who alone can prepare us to appear in His presence. Paul here quotes in abbreviated form the beautiful words of Jeremiah, so appropriate to what he has just been saying and a most fitting conclusion, in fact, to this chapter:

(Jer. 9:23, 24)   "Thus saith the Lord, Let not the wise man glory in his wisdom, neither let the mighty man glory in his might, let not the rich man glory in his riches: But let him that **31**   glorieth glory in this, that he understandeth and knoweth me, that I am the Lord which exercise lovingkindness, judgment, and righteousness, in the earth: for in these things I delight saith the Lord."

KEY WORDS AND CONCEPTS IN CHAPTER 1 AND IN PAULINE THEOLOGY

Any of these can be made a study in itself.

1. The Christian calling   2. The church, local and universal

3. The grace of God
4. Peace
5. Jesus Christ; Note the various terms: Christ Jesus, Jesus Christ, Lord Jesus Christ. [Each of these has significance in New Testament usage. Jesus, Saviour (The human aspect), Christ, the Anointed One or Messiah; Lord, the ruler or King]
6. God as Father
7. The Spirit
8. The will of God
9. Thankfulness
10. A pastoral prayer
11. Enrichment
12. Utterance
13. Knowledge
14. Gifts
15. Coming of Christ
16. Confirmation or Assurance
17. Living blameless
18. The Day of Christ (Judgment)
19. The Faithfulness of God
20. Fellowship *(koinonia)*
21. Unity
22. Christ crucified
23. Baptism
24. Preaching the Gospel *(Kerygma* and *Evangelizo)*
25. Wisdom of the world vs. the wisdom of God
26. Righteousness
27. Sanctification
28. Redemption

CHAPTER II

THE PREACHER VERSUS THE PHILOSOPHER
THE SIXTH SENSE
TWO MEN AT CORINTH

The Preacher versus the Philosopher (1-7)

The predominant theme of Paul in chapter 1—preach- **1**
ing the Gospel—is carried over into chapter 2. Paul, trained in both Greek philosophy and in Hebrew theology, determined to stick to the Gospel of Christ, avoiding "excellency of speech" or forced efforts to be

2 eloquent and to employ the catchy thought patterns of the Greek philosophers. He would never be able to build a church by attempting to exhibit his own knowledge, however profound it might be. He was not the originator of a new system of thought that was intended to replace the neat systems proposed by Epicureus, Plato, or Aristotle. Philosophers do not build churches or even society. They may well be men with *ideas,* but with a *burden* for men, no.

The enormous responsibility of dealing with men's *minds* and *souls* in terms of man's eternal destiny, made Paul humble. It sounds strange for one so well-trained, and certainly out of keeping with the pride of the typical intellectual who prides himself in his own training and achievements, to come to his people "in

3 weakness and in fear and in much trembling." His preach-
4 ing was not in the reading of cleverly-prepared "papers," quoting the big-name rabbis and philosophers of his day, but in demonstration of the Spirit and power. Too frequently today ministers think they must impress their audiences with quotations from numerous "authorities," and in far too many instances the Bible has become for them almost a forgotten book.

The purpose of Paul's technique is clear: if you quote men, the church's faith will rest on men; if you
5 demonstrate God's power in your life and preaching, the faith of the church will be founded upon the living God, the Author of the Living Word.

6 This kind of wisdom can be understood by those of mature faith, although the world would not recognize it as such, and apparently the "babes" at Corinth did not recognize it for what it was. There is a very interesting contrast here between the ones he was addressing as *teleioi* or mature Christians, (the word translated "per-
(3:1) fect" in the King James version) and the *napioi* (babes) in

16

chapter three. One's understanding of the things of God is in direct proportion to the degree of spiritual maturity.

There is also another interesting comparison between the *wisdom of God* of which Paul was speaking, and the *wisdom of this age* (world). The significant point, of **6, 7** course, is that the first is perennial, while the second passes on with the age. The contrast, in short, is between the *Wisdom of the Ages,* and the *wisdom of the age.* There is still another interesting combination in *"the wisdom (or philosophers) of this age"* and *"the rulers of* **8** *this age"* ("princes of this world"). Both the men of learning and the men of state are a part of the fleeting world order.

There is a mystical element in the Christian faith. It is **7** open to those who believe, but closed to those who do not know God. This is illustrated in the interesting sidelight Paul gives on the Gospel story of the crucifix- **8** ion, a story written some years later by the four evangelists. Had Pilate and the Roman officers known, he says, whom they were executing in 29 A.D., they would not have crucified the "Lord of glory." To them the fact of Jesus *as Lord,* was hidden. The executions of common criminals which they were accustomed to carrying out in their yearly routine, such as the two thieves crucified with Christ, were always a difficult matter, gruesome and unsavory. But this had been something quite different. The unusual character of *this* Man, apparently glimpsed for a moment by the Roman **(Matt.** centurion when it was too late—the startling fact that He **27:54)** could have been their Savior—was withheld from their normal insights. To those, however, who accepted His divine message it was clear that that Jesus whom they had slain and "hanged on a tree" was Lord both of heaven and of earth! **(Acts 5:30)**

The Sensory Versus the Spiritual (8-13)

9   Continuing from this historical reference of the crucifixion, Paul now goes on to show the difference between the ordinary senses and the spiritual sense. "Eye hath not seen nor ear heard, neither have entered **(Isa. 64:4)** into the heart of man, the things which God hath prepared for them that love him," is not really a text for a funeral sermon, though it would not be wrong to use it as such. Certainly the future glory of the saints is beyond human comprehension. More appropriately, however, Paul is stressing the fact that there are spiritual insights which cannot be gained through the "five senses." This follows so well the preceding idea that had the princes of this world, the Roman officials, *known,* they would not have crucified the Lord of glory. But they lacked the "sixth sense." That Paul is not thinking of the after-life is shown by the next statement: "But **10** God *hath* revealed them unto us by his Spirit." This is a present experience of the spiritual man.

God can never be comprehended through mere sensory knowledge. Here then is how spiritual knowledge is differentiated from earthly knowledge. The source of heavenly knowledge is God himself; the source of human knowledge is man himself. "The wisdom of the world" and "the things the Holy Ghost teaches," fall into separate categories. Spiritual things are compared (or studied) by relating them to one's spiritual insights. **11-13** To oversimplify this—we do not learn geography by studying arithmetic, and neither do we gain spiritual knowledge by studying secular books, or through sensory devices.

That, incidentally, is why so many modern techniques in religious education must be considered dubious at the best, although we do not deny the use of the sensory processes in presenting factual knowledge about God and His Word.

It is rather at the point where we attempt to use the modern idioms to lead men into a spiritual relationship with Jesus Christ where these devices fail. These, in our day, include such media as folk-rock music, drama, "happenings," and "sensitivity sessions" where the eyes, ears, and the sense of touch are exploited in bizarre ways to stir up the sensual part of man. There will never be any spiritual men emerging from this kind of "soulish," experience-centered approach. This leads us very naturally, then, to the description of the "three men at Corinth."

The Three Men at Corinth (and everywhere) (14-16)

Paul describes three kinds of men who lived in Corinth. They are representative of all men everywhere. He speaks of the *natural man,* the *carnal*   **14, 15** *man,* and the *spiritual man.* The first and third of these are described in this chapter, the second in chapter three.

The Greek words for these three types of men are very significant. The natural man is the *psuchikos,* the carnal man, the *sarkikos,* and the spiritual man, the *pneumatikos.* These terms correspond with the three-fold nature of man—*mind* (or soul), *flesh* (or body), and *spirit.* This trichotomy of the human personality is also   **(I Thess.** taught in Paul's letter to the Thessalonians.   **5:23)**

In other words, there are persons whose main life drives are centered in one or the other of these areas instead of having a balanced development like Jesus   **(Lu. 2:52)** himself had. The church at Corinth had too many of the *sarx*-centered Christians, too few of the *pneumatikoi.* The Greek world, as our modern world, was made up of many pagans who belonged to the category of the *natural man,* the man outside Christ.

19

Let us look at the two men described in this chapter.

1) *The Natural Man (psuchikos)* This is the type of person whose chief drives and motivations are "soulish" — intellectual, emotional, sensual, and earthy. The educated natural man prides himself in his human knowledge and wisdom as did the Greek philosophers and the "philosophes" of the Age of Reason. His philosophy is humanism and naturalism. Spiritual insights are foreign to him because he does not know God. Spiritual knowledge seems to insult him because it appears entirely too simple or naive. Paul uses the word **(1:21)** "absurd" (foolish in KJV) to describe his label for spiritual things. The natural man can never know God until his "sixth sense" becomes activated.

2) *The Spiritual Man (pneumatikos)* This is the man **15** who is able to "discern all things," because he sees them in their ultimate essence. He still has the use of his human senses, just as the natural man, but he also has the "sixth sense" which enables him to understand the mysteries of God. The finest synthesis of all knowledge is unquestionably made by Christian men of understanding, because they are in reality men of two worlds.

Parenthetically, this unity of all knowledge can best be achieved in the setting of Christian education, where earthly knowledge and heavenly knowledge are brought together uniquely. There is no fractionalizing of the educational process, for example, in the setting of the Christian school. Public schools may teach arithmetic well, and the Sunday school, the Bible, but only in the Christian school is knowledge brought together as a unified whole.

Paul introduces a strange paradox when he says that although the spiritual man is able to "discern (judge) all things," he himself is not discernible to those about him. Why is this? Very clearly the comparison between human knowledge and divine understanding is continued. Though the intellectual man of standing is popularly admired in every culture, and envied because of his accomplishments, even though he may be a pagan, it is the spiritual man who is really to be envied. The spiritual man has at his disposal "all the treasures of wisdom and knowledge" through Christ and divine revelation, the kind of enlightenment, in short, which makes it possible for him not only to understand and enjoy life here but also to enjoy, eventually, life beyond. A rereading here of Paul's great letter to the Colossians, chapters one and two, will be most rewarding, and will help one's understanding of the unlimited resources available to the spiritual man as opposed to those available to the merely-intellectual man. Although the intellectual man seems never able to understand the spiritual man, the spiritual man *can* understand the intellectual, and in no sense can one ever say that because a man is spiritual he depreciates the value of human knowledge. On the other hand he uses and appreciates it, but with his spiritual insights he surpasses it infinitely. (Col. 2:3)

"For who hath known the mind of the Lord?" simply **16** states the case that the infinity of the spiritual man's wisdom is tied up in the infinity of God.

In a sense, the spiritual man will always remain an enigma to the natural man who in many cases pities him for his simple, and seemingly nonintellectual approach to life, but the natural man should never forget that it is the spiritual man who has hitched his wagon to a star. He has the mind of Christ!

CHAPTER III

THE THIRD MAN AT CORINTH
CHURCH BUILDING IN THE LIGHT OF
THE FINAL JUDGMENT

The Carnal Man (1-4)

1   Paul now introduces us to the "third man at Corinth," the carnal man or *sarkikos.*

At Corinth, and everywhere, there are those who have the beginnings of the Christ-life, but who still operate on a very physical, sensual level, making their decisions on the basis of what pleases the flesh. The carnal man is still immature and undeveloped as a "babe." Someone has referred to these "babes" as "God's retarded children."

2-4   The carnal man is:

(See comment
on 2:6)

1. a creature of flesh and blood.
2. immature — a "babe" *(napios).*
3. yet he is a Christian — a babe *in Christ.*
4. in need of special diet (like a natural infant).
5. quarrelsome — engaging in petty bickering and fights ("envying and strife").
6. earthly — living on a purely human level, making decisions on the same basis as any other man.
7. factional — "Paul's my man—Apollos is my man," divided like athletic teams each rooting for its own team.

Appeal to Unity and Soundness in the
Program of Church-building (5-17)

5   Paul now makes another appeal for unity. He tries to show that church work is not a matter of leaders *competing,* but of *complementing* each other. Both of them—Paul and Apollos—were "ministers" *(diakonoi-*servants) "by whom [they had] believed." The Christians at Corinth were not on two competing teams with Paul captain of one and Apollos captain of the other. Paul uses another analogy, however, that of farm laborers working together on the same crop. "I have planted, **6** Apollos has watered; but God gave the increase." God can use an Apollos with a sprinkling can, but unless the **7** heavenly showers descend, the crop will dry up. Quite obviously, however, watering bare unseeded ground is also a futile exercise. It was Paul who had made the germination process possible in the first place. Planters **8, 9** and waterers are essentially of equal importance, and each will be rewarded according to the efficiency and faithfulness of his performance. For that reason no one **(21)** should ever rally behind particular men, but support *all* who are seriously engaged in the great task of working in God's harvest field.

Paul and Apollos were farm laborers together and the **9** Corinthians were their field (or crop). But now abruptly he changes the figure to that of a building and builders, also a very fine analogy. Paul is the masterbuilder *(architekton)* of the church through God's grace given **10** him. This probably refers to his special calling as an apostle in helping establish the church. Paul had laid a good foundation for the building—Jesus Christ. The task **10, 11** now for each church leader was to construct a good building on this foundation.

The difference in building materials represents a **12** difference of *quality.* While a farmer is most certainly interested in the quality of his production, he is also interested in *quantity* ("increase"). This was one of the main points of Christ's parable of the Four Kinds of Soil. Rewards, it appears, then, will be based on both the **(Matt. 13)** *quality* of life and the degree of fruitfulness.

The test of receiving or not receiving a reward is **(8), 13, 14** dependent on whether or not the builders, the ministers and teachers who follow, will teach the sound doctrines which he himself had preached. The seriousness of the pastor's role is emphasized. Those "materials" which have gone into the superstructure of the building—actually individual members (note verse 9, "Ye are God's **12** building")—which are "fire-proof," as represented in the gold, silver, and precious stones, will endure the test of judgment. But those materials (or members) who are represented in the wood, hay, stubble (straw), will be "burned."

It is possible, according to the teaching here, that there will be pastors and teachers, who through careless teaching and questionable building methods, will have **13-15** erected straw churches. They themselves will be saved since they built upon the true foundation, but they will not receive a reward, and their churches, or members from their churches, will be tragically lost.

Hence we note the serious responsibility of those engaged in church-building, that they constantly reevaluate their teaching and church programs lest their work may end in disaster. Paul is most certainly not referring to false teachers, as somehow being saved, but to those who were building carelessly or recklessly in seeming good faith, but whose methods and teachings were such that the end product (members) was not what they had anticipated.

On the basis of this teaching one wonders how much of today's church program must fall under the judgment of God in terms of sound Biblical construction.

We must observe that Paul is not speaking of *works* that might prove valueless or works that might save. He is speaking of every pastor's *work,* which in the final day will prove either worthy or unworthy. In chapter nine he **(9:1)** reinforces this idea when he reminds the Corinthians by rhetorical question, "Are not *ye* my *work* in the Lord?"

24

In the broadest sense, of course, one may apply this whole passage to all Christians who are "building for eternity." It is a serious responsibility for pastor and people, and there is a mutual responsibility here which both must share. Not only ministers are responsible for church-building.

On the optimistic side it is a great adventure to be engaged in helping to build the church of God, and the fruits of that labor can be greatly rewarding here and hereafter. "If any man's work abide which he hath built **14** thereupon, he shall receive a reward."

Paul concludes this solemn section on church building **16** by reminding them that this building is in reality the temple of God, a lofty name for the church. Though this has been applied frequently as meaning the individual temple of each man's body, the construction of the sentence makes it clear that he is referring to the church. "Ye (plural) are the temple (singular) of God." Their disunity was not helping to build, but to destroy the temple. It is a sin to tear down the church. "If any man defile (destroy) the temple of God, him will God **17** destroy." Later in the letter he speaks of the individual as a temple, when he says, "Know ye not that *your body* **(6:19, 20)** (singular) is the temple of the Holy Ghost, which is in you . . ." Both the body of the church and the body of the individual believer are sacred temples which need to be treated with respect and reverence.

Trusting in Man's Wisdom (18-23)

Verses 18 to 21 return us once more to the theme of chapters one and two, the wisdom of the world opposed to the true wisdom. There is no doubt that one of the major problems of this city church was how to regard the new (simple) Gospel in light of the systems of philosophy. Corinthian society with its flair for high-sounding systems of thought and sophistry had made a deep impact on those who were now part of the young church.

18   Paul boldly attacks those who seem to be wise, a very apt description of those who love to philosophize or to align themselves with popular philosophies. "Let him *become* a fool that he may (truly) be wise," suggests a kind of kneeling down process they needed to experience so that they could learn to appreciate true values. Spiritual insights come only to those who renounce "the wisdom of this world."

19, 20   In fact, contrary to popular Corinthian thought, God regards worldly wisdom as complete foolishness. Paul quotes from the book of Job and from Psalms. "It is (Matt. 4:4)   written" reminds us of Jesus' answer to Satan in the wilderness temptations and shows us that Paul, like Jesus, used "proof-texts" from the Scriptures to support his teaching. (It is still a legitimate and an effective procedure, notwithstanding modern theology's objection to finding "answers" in the Bible.) Job had said, "He (Job 5:13)   taketh the wise in their own craftiness," and the (Psa. 94:11) Psalmist, "The Lord knoweth the thoughts of the wise, that they are vain."

21-23   Thinking again of the problem of having favorites among the ministers, Paul suggests that instead of regarding them as *competitors,* they should be thought of as *contributors,* each with his specific gift.

After all, everything on earth is for man: men who influence us and thereby contribute to our lives, the world, life, death, the present, the future. Paradoxical as it may sound, all of these may in one way or other in God's time and under His sovereignty, contribute to our life and happiness and ultimate good, since we all belong to Christ, and Christ belongs to God! Later in this same (10:26)   letter he uses the expression. "For the earth is the Lord's

26

and the fullness thereof." It's all here for our good but not to be used recklessly with no regard for others. The phrase in the song, "You may have all the world, but give me Jesus," is not stating an ultimate truth, exactly, for if we have Jesus we will also inherit the earth.

CHAPTER IV

MINISTERS—JOINT MANAGERS OF GOD'S TRUTH AND FOOLS FOR CHRIST'S SAKE ON JUDGING OTHERS

Ministers as Authorized Agents of God's Truth (1-6)

"Ministers of Christ, and stewards of the mysteries of   1
God" is translated in the Goodspeed version, "Managers authorized to distribute the secret truths of God." An authorized manager or agent is expected to be trust-   2
worthy. Peter reminds us we are *all* stewards. In the   (I Pet. 4:10)
public eye a minister of Christ such as Paul was is in for public scrutiny. Paul does not reject such scrutiny, but   3, 4
says in effect—"I am not about to worry about your personal judgments on my actions. I am not aware of anything against my life and behavior, but this, of course, does not justify what I do, but the Lord is the one who really knows me." He suggests that no one   5
should pre-judge another on matters that are not really fully open to anyone's view. A minister who is disturbed by every evaluation people make of him can become depressed. Thankfully ministers are under God's direction and judgment which is a righteous judgment. All this is written primarily because of the unfair evaluations   6

27

and comparisons the Corinthians were making between Paul and Apollos, and to help them rid themselves of their childish cliques. The expression used here—"puffed up"—is used six times in this epistle: 4:6, 18, 19; 5:2; 8:1; 13:4. It means "arrogant," "exalted," "proud," "self-opinionated." The attitude of the Corinthians seems to reflect their inward carnality. Note the results of their arrogance: It

    4:6   produced factionalism

    4:18 made them judgmental

    4:19 affected their speech; their arrogant words are contrasted with spiritual power

    5:2   made them defensive of those who were wrong

A basic cause for being puffed up is:

    8:1   Knowledge (or intellectualism).

The remedy for being puffed up is:

    13:4 Christian love.

Judging Others (7-8)

7   Who makes you to differ from another? Paul asks a good question aimed at helping Christians modify their evaluations of people. What gifts one has are really no personal credit—they all come from God. He says, "You 8 have sat as kings on your own thrones of judgment." Moffat, cites the Stoic slogan taught by Diogenes, "I alone am rich, I alone reign as king," to which Paul may have been alluding. (Morris p. 79) In essence Paul is saying, "How I wish you were actually reigning with Christ and that we might sit on the throne with you as partners in Christ."

The Prestige Scale (9-13)

9   Paul was made to feel sometimes that the apostles were lowest in the prestige scale. Though called of God to a very special post, they seemed to have been

appointed to die. They were not marked for fame, but as actors on a stage (the word *spectacle* in Greek is *theatron* (theatre) they were watched by everyone—the world, angels, and men. The life of an apostle was not one of popular esteem. They were not Very Important Persons (VIP's). Rather, Paul describes them as "Fools for Christ," constantly hazarding their lives and fortunes for Christ while other Christians were seemingly on top. There is a contrast between "Ye are full" and "we are hungry" showing the difference between the well-fed Corinthians who lived a somewhat affluent life, and the apostles who had a meager subsistence. Ironically, it was they, the apostles, who were supplying them at the same time with spiritual food.

10, 13

11

(Rev. 3:17)

Here is how the apostles lived and were rated:

—lowest in the scale	—buffeted
—appointed to death	—no place to call home
—a spectacle to the world, angels, and men	—working to support themselves
—fools for Christ's sake	—reviled
—weak	—persecuted
—despised	—defamed
—hungry and thirsty	—filth and scum
—naked	

9-13

Compared to the Corinthians . . .

we are fools, but you are wise
we are weak, but you are strong
we are despised, but you are honorable
we are hungry, but you are full

10

8, 11

The apostles truly lived out the Sermon on the Mount which describes the life of the Christian,

"Being reviled, we bless
Being persecuted we suffer it
Being defamed we intreat (conciliate)."

12-13

(Matt. 5:9-11)

One gets long thoughts as he reviews these lists and

aligns them with the experiences of the typical "clergy-man" and the top religious leaders of our day. One must wonder whether *anyone* today in the affluent nations who professes to live the life of Christ is really living a life of radical discipleship, notwithstanding the lip service that is given to that phrase.

Paul most certainly knew the problems of the poor and of the working man. He had no "certain dwelling place," as also was the case of Jesus who had no place to lay his head which he could call his own. Paul labored, "working with his own hands." He made tents with Aquilla and Priscilla at Corinth. Not only did he suffer the pangs of *poverty,* but as if to add insult to injury, he was also persecuted. Yet he was not writing with a chip on his shoulder. He was not a protestor, but was able to surmount his earthly limitations. He did not mean to shame them; he was simply writing all this to warn them of wrong attitudes toward leaders like himself, who had labored faithfully in their behalf. It was not he who was being hurt. They were hurting themselves.

(Matt. 8:20)
12
14

"My Beloved Sons" (14-21)

14

Now he tries to appeal to the warm personal relationship that really existed between them. "I write not these things to shame you, but as my beloved sons I warn you." He is saying, "Fine, you boast in Apollos' abilities and teaching, but remember, that although you may have ten thousand (!) eloquent instructors like him, only I will always remain your spiritual father, 'begotten through my bringing to you the Gospel.' That is why you should follow me as you did from the beginning."

15, 16

Paul's concern for his own church at Corinth can be likened to that of a pastor who has just left a church he helped start, and who begins to discover that his charter members have rudely pushed him aside for someone else.

Paul had one he could send to them, however, Timothy, whom he could call his spiritual son and who **17** was faithful. He, Timothy, would remind them of "Paul's *ways*"—the same doctrines Paul had been preaching in every church. He could feel secure leaving his people to such a successor.

Some had been unkind enough abut Paul's prolonged **18** absence, considering this a sign of unconcern, and in this attitude they were "puffed up." He was soon to return, **20** however, and they would see demonstrated again the real power of the Gospel, which is more than "word." This would be the very best argument against the speech of the arrogant trouble-makers. When he comes, however, it will be not as a king returning from a conquest to **19** set things straight in his own realm, and to punish the servants who have become unruly in his absence. He would come as a true Christian leader "in love and meekness." There is perhaps no passage that shows in such a dramatic way Paul's great concern for the church. Though saddened for a moment and distressed because of being falsely accused, and though touched with a feeling of loneliness as a forgotten man, he rebounds here with a kindness that only the kind of love described **21** in I Corinthians 13 could possibly give.

CHAPTER V

A PURE CHURCH IN A SINFUL WORLD

Immorality in the Church (1-2)

Paul's writing to the church on a matter which had **1** been reported to him by one of the families indicates that there are times when a church leader may act justifiably on reports. The immorality in the church, incest, or living with one's mother, was one of the lowest in the scale of immoral conduct. There is some indication here that the immorality in the church was even worse than that which one might find in the pagan community.

2   Just as the Corinthians were "puffed up" in the matter of boasting about their favorite leaders, so now they were puffed up in their defense of their offending brothers and sisters. Arrogance and pride seemed to have been Corinthian sins.

2, 6   Their "glorying" was not good. It indicated that they felt they were entitled to special privileges. This is the attitude of some modern-day churches who feel they can establish their own code of congregational ethics. The egotism might be expressed in the words: "We can do this and it won't hurt us." The whole point is, sin must be dealt with. God cannot *condemn* sin in the sinner and *condone* it in the church.

Paul's Directive (3-8)

3   Paul, at long distance, was certain enough of the charges that he was ready to formulate a disciplinary procedure. It was a case where the individual—"him that hath done this deed"—must be judged by the "assembly." The process was spelled out clearly. It was not to be a matter merely of the church following democratic procedures and on the basis of common concensus to establish the *whether,* or *what,* or *how* of the situation. This was clearly outlined by their elder, Paul. Whether there was any other pastor at Corinth at the time is not certain, but at any rate, the church, acting under Paul's direction, was to carry out the disciplinary function. Though he could not be with them in person,

4   he promised he would be there with "my spirit." The

place of church leadership in the disciplinary process is **(11:34)** thus well established. For it is clear that the church itself would never have acted, even in this case of gross sin without Paul's insistence. That the action was necessary can hardly be disputed. A church without adequate oversight can actually deteriorate spiritually, but as we are to learn later, this action, well-timed under the direction of the Spirit, caused a great spiritual renewal in the Corinthian church.

The prerequisite for the Corinthian congregation, and hence for any church, when dealing with such situations, is that the body itself must have a united concern about the seriousness of the situation. The health of the body must be such that it can stand the removal of the infected "organ." A strong, positive spiritual concern is absolutely essential.

The procedure Paul outlines is simply to be:

1. "In the name of our Lord Jesus Christ"
2. "When ye are gathered together."
3. In the name of the Spirit
4. "With the power of our Lord Jesus Christ."

"To deliver such an one unto Satan" underscores the **5** fact again that mankind is divided into two groups: those who are living under the power of the Gospel and those living in Satan's realm. It suggests too that the lines are to be kept clear between the two. Immorality was one of the works of the devil and as such could not be harbored within the household of God.

The contrast of flesh and spirit is significant. Man does have a dual nature. He is a creature of two worlds. There will be a constant warfare between the flesh and the spirit. The battle which the individual could not win **(Col. 3:5)** privately must now be won publicly to teach the of- fender that the flesh must be "destroyed" or "made dead." Paul mentions this struggle in his own life. This **(Ch. 9:27)** expression may also refer to the kind of public shame such a procedure would entail, which would militate against the puffed up attitude not so much of the *offenders* as the *defenders* of sin. Better be humiliated here before the group than to be humiliated at the judgment when it is too late to be spared.

There is also another reason for dealing with this problem. Left alone, an offender could "leaven" the whole group. The matter of dealing with those who condone evil in their own lives always poses a problem for church leaders and churches. To return to the former figure, Shall a diseased organ be "surgically" removed, or shall it remain to poison the whole body with its gangrenous infection?

6, 7

Bringing into the picture "Christ our Passover" at this point is significant, since Paul is speaking of those already saved. Christ remains the Christian's Passover offering, not only as the blood of atonement, but as the blood of *cleansing.* And the relationship goes further. He is saying—You are planning to observe the Passover (Communion) feast; then make certain that those who attend have first rid their houses of leaven. The spiritual application of this Old Testament practice is clear. The leaven of malice and wickedness is contrasted with the "unleavened bread (used in the Passover Feast) of sincerity and truth."

7

(I John 1:9)

8

(Ex. 12:15)

Judging Those Within;
Judging Those Without (9-13)

The church is a unique group to be kept as pure as the private homes of the Jews who were preparing for the Passover. "Ye shall put away leaven out of your houses" was the command of Moses.

Church discipline, based on such passages as I Corinthians 5, has historically been a part of the practice of many faiths. The Anabaptists of the Reformation took this far more seriously than the other Christian groups of that day. To create a free church on the basis of voluntary membership of those committed to Christ on confession of faith was to them crucial. They could not condone the idea of a *Volkskirche* or *Landeskirche* or, in other words, a church composed of people living within certain geographic areas in the land, but who were not tied together by any spiritual ties.

To them the same door that swung inward to admit members should also swing outward, if necessary, to expel members. Membership itself was no life guarantee but needed to remain fluid in relation to the fluctuating spiritual status of its members. There are, unfortunately, churches today which have doors that swing one way only. Regardless of what their members do, they are retained in the fold. This eventually reduces a church to a "Volkskirche" with a conglomerate mixture of regenerates and unregenerates all belonging to the same body.

The question naturally arises as to what the real purpose of church discipline is. Is it for the purity of the church or for the saving of the offender's soul? The answer is, "Both," as the context here clearly indicates. And the only answer to maintaining the purity of the church is church discipline by the gathered group under faithful leadership growing out of a spiritual concern for the persons involved as well as for the body.

Far too often, as here, the offender is defended by the group under the guise of broadmindedness and brotherly love—but it is a kind of broadmindedness that seems to allow for all kinds of deviations. Instead, there needs to be a deep concern for the church and a courageous spirit that does not hesitate to take the necessary steps to rid the church of the "leaven."

35

Summarizing the whole process, it involves two simultaneous acts:

5   1. the group's delivering offenders to Satan for the destruction of the flesh so that their souls may be saved "in the day of the Lord Jesus."

8   2. the group's purging itself of malice and boastful attitudes that allow sin to exist in the congregation thereby unfitting its members to observe the communion in "sincerity and truth"

It is apparent that a church might go through the disciplinary process in a mechanical way, dutifully expelling the offender in a spirit of self-righteousness or on the basis of other wrong attitudes. Or it can be a warm, purifying process, as Paul suggests here, which will result in a stronger brotherhood.

This whole chapter cannot be fully appreciated without reading chapters 2 and 7 of Paul's second letter to the Corinthians where he makes it clear that his previous letter (either this one or the one referred to in **(II Cor. 2; 7)** verse 9), written out of love, though seemingly harsh, had accomplished what he had hoped so much it would. They had indeed profited by this disciplinary procedure. The "godly sorrow" which they had experienced had resulted in repentance leading to salvation for the offender and a clearing of themselves. These passages, taken together, form one of the most moving examples of "the church being the church" in all of church history. Church administration in the exercise of church discipline can be a beautiful experience.

9   Paul refers to a letter he had written earlier in which he had told them "not to company with fornicators." Fornication is the sin of pre-marital sex, a sin condemned in the New Testament. There is no kind of situational ethics that can legitimately make room for this, ever. Yet he explains now what he had meant in

this earlier epistle (now lost). It may be that someone in the meantime had raised some question about such an austere command of not companying with fornicators, **10** saying perhaps contemptuously that to carry this out one would have to go "out of the world." He says now that he did not intend to say that they should not keep any kind of company with fornicators or covetous or extortioners or idolaters, "for then must ye needs go out of the world." He is saying they must not keep company with one such *who claims to be a brother*—not to **11** *fellowship* with fornicators *within* the church. It was certainly obvious that if they wanted to evangelize the world, they would need to reach such on the outside. But on the other hand it was just as obvious that the church had a full agenda in just being the church, and **10-12** that it was impossible to clean up the whole world.

"With such an one no not to eat" has been **11** interpreted by some, like the Reformer, Menno Simons, and the later leaders of the Amish schism in the Anabaptist (Mennonite) faith, to mean *not to eat with offenders at the regular family table.* This method of the "ban" or "shunning" as observed to this day by the Amish church sometimes imposes awkward situations in homes where wayward children or offending husbands or wives are expelled. Mennonites have in this point not followed Simons, but have interpreted "not to eat" to mean not eating with such at the communion table. This is also the position of other churches which practice expelling of offenders. There is of course a wider application of this text which suggests that there can be unhealthy fraternizing with offending brethren and a kind of glossing over of such matters in a community that leaves the erring one proud rather than repentant. So often "sides" develop, with members within the groups either being for or against the one who has been

37

caught in the act of sin.

This also raises the question as to what lengths church discipline may go. May a brother or sister be expelled for violating regulations, of one sort or another, that do not involve any basic violation of New Testament principles? There is a danger here of abusing the Scripture to justify a wide latitude of disciplinary actions which include in some cases mere trivia, and the whims of church leaders. It also does not suggest that church leaders alone have the right to expel members who do wrong; rather it is a function of the gathered church. The basis for deciding who should be expelled, which is the final act in the disciplinary process, *is sin* and not some personal *whim.* A church cannot rightfully set up standards to judge people if those standards represent *more* or *less* than the Bible teaches and on such a basis expel people in a spirit of legalism.

On the other hand, the church *is given authority to bind and loose,* and where there is a warm, Spirit-directed concensus on matters that are not definitely in the category of the "Thou shalt's" or the "Thou shalt not's" a church may act in a way that can be strengthening. In fact, it should voluntarily assume this prerogative on important issues.

12 As a final note, the matter of *judging,* which is involved in any disciplinary action, is discussed. Isn't it always wrong for Christians to judge? many ask. The answer is, "No." We must make daily judgments on many matters, many of which involve people. Schools judge people when they set up admission standards. Businesses and industrial organizations judge people when they set standards of employment. Professional organizations and governments judge people when they set up licensing standards for the professions. Unwar-
(Matt. 7:1-5)   ranted judgment or prejudgment (basis for prejudice) is

what the Bible condemns.

Paul makes it clear that churches must have admission standards. The church is not obligated or authorized to go out and judge the world—a seeming pastime for many churchmen of our time. This is God's task. But the church does have the *prerogative, authority,* and *obligation* to deal with those "within."   **12, 13**

CHAPTER VI

LEGAL RIGHTS
COMPARED WITH MORAL LAWS

Going to Law Courts to
Obtain One's Rights (1-8)

Paul deals at this point with another practical   **1**
problem—the matter of going to law to settle disputes. "Is it possible," he asks, "that you Christians should go before a 'sinful, pagan' court to resolve your personal differences?" The paradox of the situation is that the "commonwealth of heaven"—the Christian brother-   **(Phil. 3:20)**
hood—which should really have the solution for human conflict, suddenly admits that it is unable to handle its own "civic" problems and must therefore submit them to those outside the Christian community for judgment. "Brother going to law with brother before unbelievers"   **6**
surely doesn't sound right!

The high position of saints in this life and in the   **2**
world beyond is uniquely revealed. The saints will some day judge the world! Why, then, should the world sit in judgment on the saints in trivial earthly matters?   **3**

To go to the pagan courts for a solution—to judges

4 often considered incompetent or of low esteem—was paradoxical. It was to admit that the church lacks men of sound judgment. Implicitly one finds here the suggestion that Christian men *should have* the most enlightened judgment on even earthly matters. Is there **5** "not even one" within the brotherhood who is trustworthy and wise enough to settle disputes?

This touches on a very sensitive matter, the fact that far too often church members seem to have greater esteem for the capabilities of strangers—men least known—than for their own brethren.

While this chapter does not deal directly with the church-and-state issue, it is clear that Paul regards those who are members of the civil courts as of a different character from those in the church. He refers to them as: **1** (1) "unjust" (also properly translated "unright-**(Luke 18:2)** eous")—Note that Jesus spoke of the "unjust judge"; **2** (2) belonging to the world, (implied); (3) of low esteem; **4, 6** and (4) "unbelievers."

The question of whether one may generalize on this and suggest that all who are part of the political or governmental system are of this character, is of no particular concern here. Obviously Paul was describing a pagan court in Corinth. Yet in our time we are not unfamiliar with miscarriage of justice and political intrigue. Apparently this has been true through the centuries, for Jonathan Swift, in *Gulliver's Travels,* written two centuries ago, satirized the courts and lawyers of his day in a way that was more biting than Paul's accusations. We cannot go so far, however, as to say that all who are involved in government are of this type. There have been many fine statesmen and men of character who have been involved in government and the legal system. How deeply one may become involved in governmental matters as a Christian is not the problem

40

of this chapter.

Paul now deals with the root of the whole problem, the matter of Christians quarreling among themselves. The fact that they needed *any* legal judgments raises some real question. Why should the Jewish converts who had been freed from law (Law of Moses), if any of these were involved, suddenly return to law—civil law. Or why should the Greeks, who were lovers of debate, use this cold method of settling brotherhood disputes? The Christian spirit and ethic seem to have been totally violated. Apparently the cause of the whole problem was simply greed or lust for *things*. Rather take wrong and be defrauded, he says, than to jeopardize your Christian calling. It is clear that they had not reached the high standing of the scattered Jewish Christians mentioned in the book of Hebrews, who though persecuted "took joyfully the spoiling of [their] goods." The brethren at Corinth could not tolerate being defrauded, yet they turned around and defrauded their brethren, a revenge of a peculiar sort, using evil to fight evil.

7

(James 4)

8

A Lesson in Moral Law (9-18)

What they needed was a lesson in moral law, not civil law. He subtly reminds them that the unrighteous, whatever their sin, will not *inherit the kingdom of God.* (Could it be that they had been suing for inheritance?) Then follows a list of sins, beginning with the very sin (fornication) that existed at Corinth, and about which he had just written. The folly of their position was, they were very eager to have judgment rendered on business matters by outsiders who were unjust and unbelievers, but to pass judgment themselves against professing believers who had sinned, this they were not willing to do.

9, 10

(Ch. 5)

The fact that Paul says, "such *were* some of you," carries a rebuke. They should be able to say that these

11

(II Cor. 7:1)

sins were now in the past, not still bothering them. Verse 11 deals with the whole redemptive process using the familiar Bible terms *washed, sanctified, justified,* in the name of Christ and by the Spirit of God.

Paul continues his lesson in moral law: "All things are lawful unto me, but all things are not expedient"

12

(Greek: "profitable"). One may be legal but still be wrong.

(See "Guiding Principles" pg. 62)

In stating this principle he is moving to a higher level of conduct, where one no longer distinguishes only between *right* and *wrong*, but also between *right* and *right.* There are things which may be perfectly legal—and this may well have applied to their going to law—but they are not "profitable" in terms of influence on others.

13

(Ch. 8) (Ch. 9)

There were many lawful things which Paul was forced to reject in his own life. It was lawful to eat food, but he abstained from eating certain meats for the sake of his brothers. It was lawful to marry, but Paul refrained from this for his own sake.

Paul was also concerned about the matter of Christian liberty. The Christian faith, unlike pagan religions, does not follow a system of man-made rules to guarantee his salvation, yet he is not free to do as he pleases both for what it may do to his fellowmen and to himself. "All things are lawful for me, but I will not be brought under the power of any," exposes the deception of the idea that one may have unlimited freedom in Christ. One can so easily be brought under a new slavery and be mastered by his own appetites. Eating is perfectly lawful, but one may also overeat. Sexual appetites may lead to incontinency. The body is more than a stomach and a sex urge!

14

The Christian view of the body is a lofty one. Paul here emphasizes the fact that this same Lord who is interested in the body will raise it some day—incorruptible—even as Christ was raised. It is a most unusual context for this great resurrection text. If our bodies, then, are parts of Christ's body, how can anyone take this body and join it to a harlot's body who has already **15-17** prostituted God's plan for her life? For in such union the two become one flesh. The spiritual ties with Christ **(Gen. 2:24)** make us one with him in a relationship that is far superior to any fleshly ties. The whole idea of illicit fleshly relationships is paradoxical to the whole Christian profession.

It is clear that the deepest problem at Corinth was not one that could be resolved by a pagan Corinthian court. Their hankering toward immorality and their sympathy for those who had been immoral (chapter 5) was a problem that needed the judgment both of the church and of God. In chapter five, where he deals with the problem of incest, he is saying, Put away from your church fellowship the *immoral person.* In chapter six he is saying, Put away *immorality* from your life. In fact, he says it more emphatically, "Flee from it!" Sin in its **18** essence is lawlessness, hence the folly of trying to be so precise in legal matters, when they themselves condoned lawlessness in the brotherhood.

The nature and effect of sexual sin is discussed: It is **18-20** (1) against one's own body; (2) against one's own spiritual nature; (3) against the Holy Spirit; (4) against God.

Paul seems to suggest that sexual sin involves one's own body and mind in a way that is most devastating. There are some deeply ingrained psychological involvements. The guilt experienced in violating the sexual code can literally destroy one's inner self. One may escape wicked persons by fleeing, but he can never flee from himself. It is in this sense that it becomes worse than other sins.

Our Bodies, the Temple of the Holy Ghost (19-20)

19   The high position of the human body as the temple—or innermost sanctuary of the temple, as the Greek suggests—of the Holy Ghost supercedes the psychology of the Greek philosophers. Although they believed in the duality of body and spirit, they did not see the body as more than the prison of the soul. Verse twenty strikes the key to one of the loftiest ideas of the whole New Testament: We have been bought with a **20**   price, and are now the precious possession of God! The only way to acknowledge this is by glorifying God in both body and spirit.

CHAPTER VII

ADVICE TO THE MARRIED AND MARRIAGEABLE

Advice to the Married (1-16)

Did Paul oppose marriage? Some have said yes. Critics have labeled his views as very narrow and dogmatic, regarding his writings, of course, in a purely human frame and discounting the divine element in God's Word. A careful reading, however, of this chapter—and of the entire letter—as well as of his other epistles, does not indicate that Paul ever held such a limited view. Paul did not advocate celibacy. In a later epistle he refers to **(I Tim. 4:3)** those in the end-time who falsely would teach against marriage. And later in this same letter he makes it clear that he and Barnabas, as well as the other apostles and **(Ch. 9)** brethren had the right to marry if they chose. Their apostleship or ministry did not suggest that marriage was not for the clergy. Paul's letter to the Ephesians gives one of the loftiest views of marriage that one can find anywhere.

It is evident that Paul had received some previous **1** communication from Corinth concerning the questions he now discusses. He begins: "Concerning the things whereof ye wrote unto me." Was it Paul or some members at Corinth, for example, who were suggesting, "It is good for a man not to touch a woman"? Knowing the problems they had, as noted in chapter 5, it may be that some one was suggesting, perhaps cynically, that the only alternative to the problem of immorality was simply to remain unmarried or to observe the hands-off policy *in marriage.* Verses 3 to 5 seem to indicate the possibility of such a suggestion on their part. This recalls the teachings of such widely varying religious groups as the Seventh Day Baptists of colonial Pennsylvania and the modern Father Divine cult. Paul simply restates the original command in Genesis of monogamous marriage as the only safeguard to the chastity of the human race. He is, in other words, suggesting exactly the opposite position to a rigid celibacy and "unsexuality." He is saying in verses 2 and 3 that husbands and wives need to **3** exercise a "benevolent" or open understanding toward each other in matters of sex. And while it might be good in one sense to avoid the problem of sex by simply remaining unmarried, one might simply be opening **4** himself to a completely new set of problems by remaining unmarried. The psychological interaction of husband and wife in sexual matters is very important. Each has "power" over the other in terms of eliciting or controling amorous feelings which govern or regulate the sex act. The whole point is: Do not defraud (or take advantage of) one another as one would play a game. **5**

Husbands with their naturally stronger sexual drives need to be considerate, and wives, in consideration of these drives, must not defraud or cheat their spouses of their conjugal rights. The marriage union itself implies that neither spouse is sole possessor of his or her own body, or putting it more positively, both partners must share mutually in this physical expression of married love in a way that contributes significantly to each other.

Wives sometimes withhold marital privileges as a punitive gesture to bring their husbands to terms on some point of disagreement, or they may use this method as a means of wrenching some concessions from them. Or the reverse could be true about husbands. The only kind of moratorium on the sex act, however, that is justifiable or psychologically workable is that which represents a mutual agreement "for a time" for some stipulated or highly motivated reason, barring at this point physical reasons or other understandable interventions. The concept of "sublimation" in psychology may be applied here. Sublimation is substituting to advantage an activity of a higher level for that of a lower. In this case it would be abstaining from the (lower) physical function for a time, for the sake of performing more zealously the (higher) spiritual function, as one might, for example, abstain from food for a time (in fasting) because of some deep spiritual concern. However, such abstinence, prolonged unnecessarily, might only open the door for Satan to suggest some illicit liaison under the pretense that the biological drives must be satisfied.

6 Paul is simply suggesting here a workable formula or concession and is not necessarily imposing a rule that would fit every situation. His statement here, that he is speaking "not of commandment" but by "permission"

as well as his later statements that it is he that is
speaking and not the Lord, does not mean that at these   (12, 25)
points the Bible is not inspired or that what Paul is
writing was of a different level or quality of inspiration.
It simply means that at these points there had been no
explicit statement by Christ. Paul's judgment is in
keeping with the commandments of the Lord and serves
as an amplification or application of principles set forth
by Christ. This is very significant, in fact, as it gives us
some clue as to how one may apply the Scriptures
pragmatically in a way that is in keeping with the Word.

There are some who like himself have handled the   7
problem best by remaining unmarried, but people differ
and one must recognize the differing "gifts" of people.
For some, to remain unmarried, as already suggested,
might *create* rather than *solve* problems.   7, 8

It is certainly better to marry than to "burn," that is,   9
to be tortured by unsatisfied desire, or caught by
unrestrained passion. This kind of view of marriage may
seem to degrade marriage to a very ignoble level, but it is
simply facing up to the hard facts of life realistically.
Failure to do so has ended in shipwreck for many homes
and lives.

Permanence of the Married State (10-11)

Speaking to the married now, Paul issues an authori-   10
tative command which he states has been commanded   (Matt. 19:6)
by the Lord. He is presumably speaking here of those
marriages where both partners are Christians. "Let not
the wife depart from her husband ... and let not the   11
husband put away his wife." Jesus had said, "What
therefore God hath joined together, let not man put
asunder." He is protecting himself against misunderstanding on the permanence of marriages already contracted lest those who read his letter would misunder-

47

stand from what he has just said previously to the unmarried, that it would be good to abide in the single state. Marriage was to be indissoluble, and Paul did not want anyone to justify separation on the basis that he had taught them that celibacy was better. Wives were not to depart, and husbands were not to "put away" their wives, the latter expression of which can be best understood in terms of the Old Testament code. In the event a separation takes place, however, whatever the circumstances, the parties are to remain unmarried so that the door of reconciliation will always be open. The same idea is expressed later in the chapter where he writes:

(39)   The wife is bound by the law as long as her husband liveth; but if her husband be dead, she is at liberty to be married to whom she will . . .

12   Paul now speaks "to the rest," those involved in mixed marriages brought about when one or the other partner became converted from paganism or Judaism. It is a problem that has confronted young churches on the missionary frontier at various times and places in the history of the church. It is a problem confined not only to missionary churches. In light of Paul's teaching in his **(II Cor.** second letter to the Corinthians on not being "yoked **6:14-18)** together with unbelievers," one might ask why Paul did not apply that rule here and demand the believing husband or wife to become "unyoked." The point is, of course, that in his second letter where he speaks of the unequal yoke he was warning chiefly against being yoked together with unbelievers in heathen temple worship, a problem which he deals with at length in chapters 8 and 10. The principle can, however, be applied on a much wider scale, although it is evident he did not apply it here.

And while he was not advocating that those already

married should become unyoked, he also made it clear later that those unmarried who were contemplating marriage should marry "only in the Lord."

Paul's answer then to this whole problem in brief is: If your unbelieving partner consents to remain with you, do not part. If, on the other hand, he or she departs, there is nothing you can do about it. Rather than cause undue tension that cannot be resolved, it may be better to separate, for "God has called us to peace." **15**

12, 13

One can easily imagine that separation may in some instances have been the way of peace, judging from the animosity of some of the citizens in Corinth against Paul and Sosthenes. One can easily believe that there may have been homes where this tension might have been quite strong, especially where neighborhood sentiments might have come into play. Jesus himself had predicted that accepting Him might in some cases bring division into homes, so that this was not merely an academic question. **(Acts 18)** **(Matt. 19:29)**

As indicated Paul had not advised believers to marry unbelievers, and here is where the teaching on the "unequal yoke" would still apply. But if the conversion took place after marriage, the "higher law," would be, Stay married unless it becomes completely impossible to do so.

Paul's word distinguished from the Lord's, as suggested earlier, simply indicates that there had been no specific command at this point from the Lord. His command here is simply an amplification of Christ's command. It also indicates that Paul was honest enough to make clear that the Lord in his ministering had not specifically spoken on this point. **12** **(Matt. 5:32)**

Paul discusses the matter of the validity of the marriage union when it was contracted prior to conversion. By saying, Don't break up the marriage formed in **14** the pagan or unconverted state and performed by pagan or Jewish rites, Paul simply says that marriages performed in sub-Christian cultures are still valid or legal in the sight of God and men. The principles of marriage and the Sabbath antedate the Law (and, of course, the New Testament) by many centuries. They were primeval commands binding on mankind for all time and basic to the purity and sanctity of the race.

The fact then that either partner has become a Christian is no valid reason for separation or divorce—rather, a reason for staying together, since the "unbelieving husband is sanctified by the wife and the unbelieving wife is sanctified by the husband." Thus the unbelieving partner (or the children) may have the opportunity to fall under the Christian influence of the believing partner. They become "sanctified," or "made holy" through them. Paul is apparently suggesting that there is a kind of special blessing afforded by one or the other being a Christian which covers or hallows the other through close fellowship. He also says, by staying together the unbelieving partner may be won for Christ. Paul's constant aim was to win others for Christ, to work for their profit, to edify rather than destroy. His approach was always positive. It is interesting to note in this connection that the Reformed doctrine of "covenant children," derived in part from this passage, considers that any child born into a home where one or the other parent is Christian is able to claim the "covenant blessing." Only where one or both parents are Christians are they permitted to attend Reformed Christian schools.

16
(I Pet. 3:1)

14 But the expression "else were your children unclean" may signify also legitimacy. Children born to pagan parents, even where both are pagan, are not illegitimate, so long as there is a legal marriage contract publicly registered and recognized.

Abiding in One's Calling (17-24)

One of the chief guiding principles of happy living is   **17**
to accept one's position in life whatever the situation
may be. This is not to suggest a kind of Stoicism in
which one grits his teeth and bears it, but it means
accepting every situation as an opportunity for grace to
work. It is a word needed for our day when militant
groups are suggesting that the only answer to any
problem is immediate action to end the injustices. Under
this slogan even acts of violence are justified and the
New Testament teaching on suffering seems to be a
forgotten theme.

Those Jews who had become Christians—and appar-   **18**
ently many Hellenistic Jews had—were not in any way
to try to obliterate their ethnic status or to despise their
former rites. And the Gentiles, just to please some
Jewish brethren, should not submit to Jewish initiation
rites. For Christians national or racial distinctions are
not important, but obedience to God. The different   **19**
national and racial groups must learn to accept each   **(cf. Gal. 5:6)**
other, whether Jew or Gentile. Comparing the outward
rite of circumcision with the "commandments of God,"
indicates the change from the Old Covenant to the New
Covenant, with the Old being either fulfilled in or
superceded by the New. Paul was serving at a critical
point of history when the Christian faith was replacing
the Hebrew faith. Paul expands his idea of abiding "in the   **20**
same calling wherein he was called" to the social context.
Whatever your social condition or situation when you   **21**
become a Christian—do not think you must immediately   **24**
alter it. If you are a slave, work—for the time being—in
that context. If you see your way clear to freedom, then
use that for your springboard for service for the Lord.
Goodspeed's rendering of this text suggests even more:
"Even if you can gain your freedom, make the most of

51

your present condition instead." In other words, there might be cases where a Christian slave might be able to perform some greater service by remaining in slavery, such as winning his master for Christ, in which case he could then enjoy his freedom in triumph. In no case, however, was Paul suggesting that slavery was a defensible institution. He was simply trying to work within the structures of the society in which he lived in a way that would build rather than tear down. He was not a crusader for a new movement that was to overthrow evil social institutions or the "establishment."

22

The whole concept of freedom—so dear to mankind—is grossly in need of exploration. For men outside Christ are in reality in slavery to sin. And that which men of the world call freedom may be their death. Though they may endure persecution, suffering, and oppression from those who are evilly disposed toward the things of God, in Christ there is a kind of freedom that is priceless. For in reality, even though one may be physically a slave, he is really the Lord's freedman, and when he becomes a Christian, he paradoxically becomes Christ's slave.

Paul is saying, "You have been bought by your new slavemaster with the price of redemption, do not unwittingly, then, become a slave to men in the myriad ways in which one may become enslaved."

23

Advice to the Marriageable (25-38)

25

Paul is giving his own judgment as one who has "obtained mercy of the Lord to be faithful," concerning the question of remaining unmarried. That is why this again is better considered good advice in terms of expediency in the present situation, than a direct commandment of the Lord.

Measured in terms of the times (55 A.D.), Paul "supposed" it was better to remain unmarried. The very way in which this is proposed—and by inspiration placed here—indicates the way in which Christians in all ages must try to find answers in matters where there is no "Thou shalt," or "Thou shalt not." Marriage is certainly **26** not a "Thou shalt." So then there may be times when it is advisable and times when it is not. By the same token celibacy cannot be imposed on anyone.

Applying this principle in the broadest sense, then, although remaining single may have been wisest for that **27** specific period of stress and persecution, there are no grounds here for *separating* to fit into this expediency.

They would certainly not sin by marrying, but in **28** those critical times they might have some troubles from which they might be spared.

Whether Paul seemed to sense a soon return of the **29** Lord, or whether he was merely pointing out some precautions, he does state some *principles* here that are worthy of consideration. Single persons have, in many respects, less to be concerned about than married people, and even if one is married, he dare not be so tied down that he cannot serve Christ. Time is short, and, using his admonition to the church at Ephesus, one must "redeem **(Eph. 5:16)** the time for the days are evil."

One must always live in this same context, since **30** sorrows and troubles, as well as joys, are but temporal and fleeting. Likewise, one must never become so earthbound with possessions that his central interests and energies are diverted. Goodspeed translates this "... and those who mix in the world, as though they **31** were not absorbed in it." Paul states here a grand principle for all Christians: Use the world where it can serve a noble purpose in furthering God's kingdom, but don't abuse it." For, as we know, the world system is fleeting and will pass away.

Being married involves certain cares which cannot **32**

lightly be laid aside. Paul himself could hardly have carried on his own rigorous evangelistic program and the founding of new churches had he been married. Obviously one who is married must rightfully be concerned with his own family. A minister, for example, cannot walk away from his family under the guise that he must "seek first the kingdom of God" and be separated for long periods of time from his rightful paternal responsibilities. In such cases where a man feels called to some special service of this sort, he had better decide first whether he should get married. This is part of counting

33 the cost. Once married he will obviously rightfully try to please his wife.

34 The same holds for a married woman trying to please her husband and being concerned with family affairs.

35 Paul is simply trying to help people think carefully through the whole matter of being married and the responsibilities it entails, versus the spiritual advantages the single person has. He is not trying to confuse them or keep them from marrying. His whole objective is to help them to find such a station in life that will allow them to "attend upon the Lord without distraction."

He speaks now of fathers who had marriageable daughters and were not settled in their minds as to what responsibilities they had toward them. In those days **36-38** fathers had a special authority in giving away daughters, the symbolic gesture of which is still retained in modern wedding ceremonies. Paul uses a very poetic expression—"If she pass the flower of her age"—to denote being fully developed or mature and therefore ready for marriage. To withhold from such the right to marry would be an unduly harsh paternal imposition. Some think Paul is referring to marriage partners who were contracting "spiritual marriages" with a previous agreement to abstain from conjugal relations, but the former inter-

pretation seems more acceptable. The problem, there- (See com-
fore, was not specifically a Corinthian problem. Paul ment on
says, thinking again of the strenuousness of the times, if verse 1.)
a father chooses to give his daughter in marriage,
fine—"he sinneth not" and "doeth well," and on the other
hand he that keeps "his virgin doeth well." In his own
personal judgment, keeping her was the best choice.

Permanence of the Marriage Contract, Restated (39-40)

Paul closes chapter 7 by restating his views on **39, 40**
marriage, which earlier he had observed was the com- **10**
mandment of the Lord.

> "The wife is bound by law as long as her husband
> liveth; but if her husband be dead, she is at liberty to be
> married to whom she will; only in the Lord."

There is one condition to marrying the second time
(or the first time), that he must marry "in the Lord."
We are all familiar with second marriages of respected
Christians who made a choice outside the body of
believers. This destroys good Christian influence in any
community.

Again he expresses his opinion that he feels widows
will be happier to remain unmarried. He feels that this is
not only his own personal judgment but the will of the
Spirit which is his constant personal possession to give
him wise direction.

SUMMARY OF THE TEACHINGS OF
I CORINTHIANS 7

1. Living singly is fine if a person chooses this course, **1, 2, 9**
   but marriage is a safeguard against promiscuity and
   immorality.
2. A husband and wife must have mutual understand- **3-5**
   ings and cannot deprive each other of lawful

marriage relations.

7, 8,
32, 35

3. There *are* advantages in remaining unmarried, but celibacy is not a superior state.

12-16

4. Separation is not required simply because one becomes a Christian and the other remains pagan.

14

5. Both partners do not need to be Christians to make the marriage legitimate.

17-24

6. You do not need to alter your social status just because you become a Christian.

35-38

7. A father may or may not give his marriageable daughter in marriage.

10, 11, 39

8. Marriage is for life.

25-28

9. The times do affect the decision to become married, but should not be the sole basis for determining whether or not one should become married.

29-31

10. One should not make marriage the ultimate achievement or goal in life.

39

11. The ideal marriage partnership is "only in the Lord."

CHAPTER VIII

CHRISTIAN "SITUATIONAL ETHICS"—A STUDY IN CONSCIENCE, PERSONAL CONVICTION, AND BROTHERLY RELATIONS

Eating Meat Offered to Idols (1-13)

Paul now turns to another problem facing the young church. This was eating meat offered to idols. The principles established here are so comprehensive that if followed by all Christians would solve many problems facing the church.

The matter of "touching things offered unto idols"

involved three specific situations (including the discussion in chapter 10):

1. eating sacrificial meat *knowingly* at a banquet at a pagan temple or in a place connected with idol worship.   **10**

2. eating sacrificial meat *unknowingly* as a guest in a pagan home.   **(10:27)**

3. eating sacrificial meat *knowingly* as a guest in a pagan home, after having been informed by one sitting by that it was meat which had been offered to idols.   **(10:28)**

The problem involved four groups of persons: (1) the enlightened Christians who knew that idols "were nothing in this world"; (2) new converts to Christianity who had an oversensitive (weak) conscience; (3) Gentiles, or pagan townsfolk; and (4) Jews.   **4, 7**   **(10:32)**

Whether the problem was immorality (chapter 5), or eating sacrificial meat (chapters 8 and 10), or wrong attitudes towards leadership (chapters 1, 3, 4), the carnal Christians at Corinth always professed to know the answers. Paul says, however, "If anyone thinks he knows all the answers (Taylor), he still has a lot to learn" (Phillips). Instead of their knowledge mellowing their attitudes toward those who were supersensitive about eating "contaminated" meat, their certainty about the folly of idol worship tended to make them arrogant and reckless. "If it doesn't hurt me, it can't hurt anyone else," seemed to summarize their attitude. Knowledge in itself "puffeth up." If they were really concerned about church-building (edifying), then what they needed was brotherly love. Love is always the key to good church relations and to good church-building. It is the basis of all wholesome conscientious attitudes toward all men in all situations.   **2**   **1**

Knowledge of God (as the one true God) is impor-   **3**

(Gal. 4:9) tant, but this can be very academic. *Loving* Him and having the assurance of God's presence in one's life is far more essential.

4-6 While these enlightened Christians knew that an idol was *nothing,* and that there was but one true God, not everyone in the city of Corinth had reached their own high level of monotheism. In fact, they themselves were still not so far removed from idol worship that they had any reason for feeling proud, and in this pride to trample rough-shod over the consciences of those who were not enjoying the fullness of their freedom in Christ. Some of these still had a secret awe of idols. "Through being long accustomed to idols [they] still eat meat that has been sacrificed to them as really offered to an idol, and their consciences, being oversensitive, are troubled" (Goodspeed). For such to continue to eat this meat would "defile" (or essentially "destroy") their consciences. It reminds one of those in contemporary Christendom who have become converted from heathendom but who have never been quite able to shake off some of the former practices which from childhood they had come to venerate.

Writing to the Romans later on the same problem, (Rom. 14:23) Paul said, "He that doubteth is damned (or condemned) if he eat, because he eateth not of faith: for whatsoever is not of faith is sin." In short, one who disregards his personal conviction sins.

This establishes a very interesting principle of conduct; namely, that in one's own private acts one must always be aware of the effects they may have on three specific groups of persons: unbelievers, those of other faiths, and his own brethren. In making decisions on matters that in themselves seem perfectly right and where one is assured of the correctness of his own position, he must be careful that he does not become arrogant, as did the Corinthians in their position. One should always think twice to make certain his actions are not misunderstood or cause others to stumble. "Stumble," as used in these passages, means *to cause others to lose out with God.* Paul makes it clear that apparently harmless acts can be wrong, judged by the high ethic of spiritual concern for others. This is a different kind of situational ethics from that which Jews or pagans knew, or that proposed by the situational ethicists of our day.

Jewish ethics was grounded in legalism, which simply made every act either right or wrong in terms of the Mosaic Law. Modern situational ethics makes each act right or wrong in terms of people or situations, presumably basing it on so-called "love." The Jewish legalists had forgotten true God-love, which Christ had clearly stated was the fulfilling of the law in terms of the God relationship and the man relationship. Thus while the Jews stressed law without love and the situational ethicists of our day stress love (so-called) without law, the Christian believer stresses *law fulfilled in love.*

The Corinthians were weak in both law and love. (1, 2, 3) Their knowledge was grounded not in a knowledge of God but in mere human knowledge or reason, and their love toward God and men was lacking. The only sound ethics is that which is strong in both its vertical dimension with obedience to God's law through love, and in its horizontal dimension with respect for the human personality through *Agape,* or Christian love.

Meat in itself has no moral quality, so whether one eats or doesn't eat it makes him no better or no worse.

But Paul warns those who were using their new-found 8 freedom recklessly. While the eating of the sacrificial meat would not necessarily hurt them, their flouting of this freedom before those of weak conscience might 9 cause them to stumble. There were in reality *two kinds* of "weak brothers" about whom they needed to be concerned: those who ate the meat *reluctantly*, thus violating their own conscience, and those who themselves did not eat the meat because of conscience but stumbled at watching others eating it who had no conscience on the matter. It also involved the conscience of the stronger brother who had seemingly little regard for either of these two. While the one who ate the meat reluctantly sinned against *his own conscience*, the strong, enlightened brother sinned against the consciences of *his weak brethren*, causing them to become "emboldened" to violate their weak consciences. It is interesting to note that the Greek word here for "emboldened" means "edified." Rather strikingly, Paul, whose chief concern is the edifying (building) of the church, warns them that in this case they were building in the wrong direction—actually "unbuilding." In short, eating with a *loose* conscience as in the case of the strong brother is bad, and eating with a *bothered* conscience as in the case of the weak brother is bad.

Even if one could do all this with a clear conscience within the brotherhood itself, there were still others for whom they were responsible. This included pagans and Jews, both of whom might be surprised to see Christians still eating meat offered to idols after their conversion.

Paul himself was in a unique position to understand this particular problem of the Corinthian church. He himself had grown up in a Jewish home where they had many restrictions on the eating of meats, and he had laid all of these aside for Christ, who was the fulfillment of the Law. In his new-found liberty he felt free from these former restraints, but some of these who were former pagans seemingly did not enjoy the same full liberty in Christ. Yet it was for these that Paul made his urgent appeal for charity.

Paul was quite emphatic in his position, asking the "puffed up" Corinthian brethren how they could so nonchalantly eat meat when a man's soul was at stake. He calls it sin against the brethren and against Christ.

One can hardly overemphasize the high place Paul gives in all his writings to conscience. He speaks at one place of always exercising himself to have a conscience "void of offence toward God and toward men." To the Romans he wrote, "I say the truth in Christ, I lie not, my conscience also bearing me witness in the Holy Ghost." His, of course, was a conscience always tied to the Word, to Christ, and to Holy Spirit guidance. He did not merely call his personal opinion conscience. Conscience anchored in true knowledge of God and conditioned by love (note verse 1 again) cannot help bringing positive results in terms of church-building. (Acts 24:16) (Rom. 9:1; I Tim. 2:7)

Paul's concluding statement becomes a guiding principle not only for Paul but for all Christians for all time—"Wherefore if meat make my brother to offend, I will eat no flesh while the world standeth, lest I make my brother to offend (fall)." In chapter 10 he summarizes the whole matter so beautifully when he lays down this comprehensive rule of conduct: "Give none offence, neither to the Jews, nor to the Gentiles, nor to the church of God." He is saying, Live a life that those inside and outside the church will not stumble at your misbehavior—but more, Seek not your own profit, "but the profit of many, that they may be saved." **13** (10:32, 33)

The Importance of Paul's Word on Eating Meat

Coming as it does right in the middle of this letter, chapter eight seems to be a crucial part of the letter. It establishes an ethical code which might well be termed the highest level of Christian conduct. Or one may speak of this as the *Code of Christian Situational Ethics.*

As stated earlier, the formula for Christian conduct is not one of individual choice, nor is it based merely on cause and effect, which will obviously shift with circumstance. It must always be motivated and controlled by the high expedient of glorifying God and edifying the church. It is at this point where the whole idea of Christian expediency (not mere diplomacy), which is above and beyond mere legalism, is elevated to the very highest level. It is not simply a matter of trying to avoid conduct which might *endanger* someone, or of engaging in conduct that might be self-advantageous, but it should be of the sort which will *enhance* the other person's relationship with God. This is the highest standard of conduct stated in the Bible.

In a day of relativism and situational ethics, when men insist that there are no fixed rules of conduct to govern human behavior, it is good to know that the Bible does not leave us stranded without some principles that have abiding experience. The following is an attempt to list some of these.

Some Guiding Principles of Christian Conduct, or New Testament "Situational Ethics" (As derived from I Corinthians and other New Testament Writings)

Some representative supporting texts:
(Gal. 5:19-21; Rev. 22:15)

There is some obvious overlap as we attempt here to state the various principles the New Testament proposes, but we list them as follows:

1. Things wrong in themselves are always wrong. The New Testament gives us a number of specific lists of sins after which it states explicitly that they who do such things "cannot inherit the kingdom of God."

(I Thess. 5:22; (I Cor. 8)

2. Whatever is questionable or having the appearance of evil should be avoided.

(I Thess. 5:21)

3. All options should be tested and only the best chosen. The most difficult choices in life are often

not between the *good* and the *bad,* but between the
good and the *best.* As Paul points out in this chapter, **(I Cor. 8)**
there is often a choice between *right* and *right,* if the
good of the church and our brothers is to be
considered.

4. Acts that are in themselves right or "legal" are **(I Cor. 6:12;**
not always "expedient" (profitable, or advisable) in **10:23)**
terms of influence on others' conscience. Modern
situational ethics says *wrong* may sometimes be *right,*
while Christian situational ethics says that *right* may
sometimes be *wrong.*

5. Any acts which may cause others to stumble, **(Rom. 14)**
though themselves harmless, should be avoided. One
should always be considerate of the other man's **(I Cor. 8:13;**
eternal welfare. **10:24)**

6. Anyone who performs an act that is doubtful **(Rom. 14:23)**
automatically condemns himself.

7. If anyone feels free to do things which those **(I Cor. 8:12)**
who are influenced by him may consider wrong, he
sins against them and against Christ.

8. Whatever one does or says should contribute to **(I Cor. 10:23;**
church-building. **14:5, 12)**

9. Whatever one does should be done to the glory **(I Cor. 10: 31, 33)**
of God, with the end in view of saving men.

10. If one knows to do good and fails to do it, he **(James 4:17)**
commits sin. (This is the sin of omission.)

CHAPTER IX

A MINISTER'S RIGHTS AND RESPONSIBILITIES

"Are You Not Mine? Am I Not Yours?" (1-2)

(Phil. 1:7)

There are certain places in Paul's writings where he seems to open up his heart and speak as man to man. Chapter 9 is one of these. No one who reads his writings can escape the feeling that Paul was truly a man with an "enlarged heart," as he had written to the church at Philippi. For those who at times questioned his authority and methods he reminded them once and again that he had been called as an Apostle "by the will of God." He could claim the special sanctions that fitted those who were called for this great task. He had not been one of the original Twelve, but was called later in a miraculous way to be the bearer of the Glad Tidings to the Gentiles. It was on the road to Damascus that he had seen Jesus, one of the qualifications of a certified apostle. He reminded them too, no doubt with deep emotion, that they—the Christians at Corinth—were his "work in the Lord." They were his harvest, his building. It is a rewarding experience for a pastor to look into the faces of his parishioners and see among them those who represent the fruit of his labors.

1

(3:9)

2

"If there are those who say I am not their apostle," we may paraphrase, "I am certain that I am yours. In fact, you are my official seal to certify me as an apostle."

Have We Not the Right to
Eat and to Drink . . . ? (3-18)

3

After trying to answer the critics who questioned Paul's right *to be* an apostle, he now attempts to meet the arguments of those who questioned his rights *as* an apostle. His discussion here follows closely on the theme of chapter 8 on one's acts in respect to others, only here he speaks of personal *rights* rather than personal *liberty*. Paul was also willing to forego certain *rights* as well as liberty for the sake of the Gospel. He reminds them that he has the same rights as other apostles to eat and to drink and to "lead about a wife." That is, he has the **4, 5** right to expect support for himself and for a wife as he travels about, if he chooses to marry. It is not an unreasonable demand. He and Barnabas were not necessarily required to follow a gainful vocation to maintain themselves. What he says from this point on seems to apply to all those who are ordained to preach the Gospel. A minister does have the right to be a "full-time" pastor or evangelist and to expect support **6** from those he is called to serve. "The laborer is worthy **(Luke 10:7)** of his hire."

Paul then uses several illustrations to reinforce his point. The soldier, for example, does not go to battle at **7** his own expense. The vinedresser eats some of the fruits of his own labors. Even the shepherd (in Greece usually a slave, in those times) is allowed to use milk from the flock he tends.

He is not trying to prove his point only "as a **8** man"—that is from mere human logic. "It is written" in **9** the Scriptures that this should be so. The Law of Moses had made provision even for animals who served their masters: "Thou shalt not muzzle the mouth of the ox that treadeth out the corn." If God takes care of oxen, He **10** surely makes provision for His servants. This was written, in fact, to teach men the principle that the laborer should be rewarded. Those who plow and those who thresh do so in hope of some reward.

If a farmer rightfully expects to reap a natural harvest **11** from his fields, why shouldn't the minister working with God's "husbandry" reap from his field. It can certainly

65

not be wrong for a minister to "reap your carnal things" (money, or cash in kind) for his spiritual service. This is not charity or a dole that people are obligated to give to a minister as a means of subsistence. It is a just reward. A

12 minister and his family do need to live just as other people, and as long as there are "others"—door-to-door salesmen, storekeepers, organizations of one sort or another, daily exercising this "power" over his members, why should it be so grossly improper for a minister to have his own fair share of their material things for his spiritual services?

In a sense a minister is also selling a product, but Paul wants it clearly understood that he is not trying to use his powers of persuasion merely to extract from them some material gain. He would rather suffer privation than to have it said that he was using his work among them for material gain, and thereby "hinder the Gospel of Christ." He reminds them further that the priests and Levites of the Old Testament times had received their

13 living from people's tithes. Just so "the Lord ordained" (planned) that under the New Covenant those who preach should also receive their living from the people they serve.

14 To make a practical comment here, it should be noted that if today churches were to abide with even the mere legal level of the Law and observe the principle of the tithe (tenth), it would take only ten wage earners to support a pastor. This is presupposing, of course, that the pastor and his family would be living on an economic level comparable to that of the average parishoner.

15 Again, however, Paul backs modestly away from his own proposal, not to negate what he has just said, but simply to make it clear that he would rather *die* than to create the feeling that he was pressuring them to his advantage, a charge which some of the false teachers and critics at Corinth would have been quick to take up against him. He could glory in his calling but this was not his desire. The calling of the minister is not one of **16** high public honor, the kind of social status many prominent pastors of our day seem to enjoy. It is not a *profession* which a man follows for personal glory or advantage or even for personal satisfaction. It is instead a *responsibility* one assumes when he is called of God, and in such a divine setting a minister can exclaim with Paul, "Woe is unto me if I preach not the Gospel!"

Paul makes it clear that he is not doing this by **17** constraint or by compulsion, but voluntarily; only in this way can he hope to receive a reward. If he performs the task unwillingly, he will fall under condemnation. Summing this up, then, the minister of the Gospel serves voluntarily, not of necessity, and not for material gain, but in fulfillment of a divine vocation which is inescapable.

What is his real reward then? It is that without charge he can give them the message God expects him to give. Paul was not tied to them by any financial strings. He **18** was their servant but by his own choice. His highest ambition was to win people for Christ, pay or no pay. This was the full measure of his sincerity.

Becoming All Things to All Men (19-23)

Paul was not the type of person to spend hours in **19, 23** seminars on "methods." His methods grew out of his zeal and his love and burden for people. So concerned was he that he tried to adjust himself to all men, whether Jew or Gentile that he "might by all means, save some." Becoming "all things to all men," did not imply, however, that he would stoop to the level of committing sin with them in order to gain church

67

members. In the modern context it does not imply that a pastor should drink the social drink with those who drink or run with people to their many places of amusement in order to impress them that he is "human." Paul is simply speaking of adapting one's techniques for the sake of communicating the Gospel. It meant refraining to eat meat for the sake of the man with the "weak conscience," that he "might gain the weak." It meant, too, foregoing their support for the sake of avoiding anyone's stumbling over this.

(II Cor. 11:7-12) In Paul's second letter to the Corinthians where he reviewed his own financial status in connection with his instructions on giving, he reveals some of the trials and tensions he experienced. He wrote:

> "Have I committed an offense in abasing myself that ye might be exalted, because I have preached to you the Gospel of God freely? I robbed other churches, taking wages of them, to do you service. And when I was present with you, and wanted, I was chargeable to no man: for that which was lacking to me the brethren which came from Macedonia supplied: and in all things I have kept myself from being burdensome unto you, and so will I keep myself. As the truth of Christ is in me, no man shall stop me of this boasting in the regions of Achaia. Wherefore? because I love you not? God knoweth. But what I do, that I will do, that I may cut off occasion from them which would desire occasion; that wherein they glory, they may be found even as we."

The indication is clear that rather than to impose a burden on the reluctant and critical Corinthians, Paul would take the freely-given support of the other churches in the province. This was a matter which he felt free to make known publicly, not to belittle the Corinthians, but as a challenge to them and to help silence the critics.

We gather from this, too, that in the church's total ministry of giving to ministerial support, it may be necessary for some churches to carry the financial burden of others which seem less willing to participate or which may be less capable. It seems to suggest, too, that there should be some measure of equality in the entire system of ministerial aid. There is nothing in all of the New Testament which lends any support to the idea that pastors of large churches, such as in the metropolitan and suburban centers, should receive greater financial support than those who are called to serve in the remote regions or in small rural churches. The church of our time has much to learn about giving equitable ministerial support, and ministers have much to learn by way of frugal living geared not to the standard of their wealthier constituents but in the direction of those who have a low income. At the least, the minister's demands for a comfortable living should not hinder the spread of the Gospel to the more remote and more sparsely settled regions where the standard of living may be lower.

"So Run That Ye May Obtain" (24-27)

The Christian life is rewarding to *all* who dedicate **24** themselves to its tasks. While in a race only one wins, in this race *all* can win. As the athlete undergoes certain rigors and privations for the sake of winning, so in the Christian race there needs to be rigorous self-discipline. All the athlete can hope to get in the end is a laurel wreath which will finally disintegrate, but the Christian crown is eternal.

Paul's analogy is good. As the track-runner or fighter **25** in the arena is fully prepared for his contest, so Paul determined to be adequately prepared for his task. Self-imposed disciplines on his own body ("self-buffeting") were necessary to win in the end. It would be a shame if he, a minister of the Gospel, after having preached for years to save others, would in the end be lost himself. In spite of clever theorizing and mishan-

69

dling of Scriptures to prove some form or other of "eternal security," *falling away,* or being "rejected" (cast away) is not an impossibility for the Christian. It is a haunting reality, thankfully offset, however, by the grace of God and the promise of victory through Christ.

CHAPTER X

SIN AND ITS CONSEQUENCES
THE PROMISE OF VICTORY
COMMUNION AND QUESTIONS OF CONSCIENCE

Israel in Its High Position Fell (1-12)

1

(Ex. 13:21)

Continuing somewhat in the same theme of the closing verses of the previous chapter, Paul reminds the Corinthians of the seriousness of their calling and the possibilities of falling. He goes back to the story of Israel in the wilderness. They too had been followers of God and had had the full evidence of God's approval. They were "under the cloud," the symbol of God's leading and protection. And as a special seal "they all underwent baptism as followers of Moses." (Twentieth Century

2
3, 4
(Psalm 78)
(John 6)
(Ex. 16:15)

New Testament). They were all fed spiritual food (manna) and were given spiritual drink from the Rock, which interestingly is here identified as Christ. They had all the earmarks and blessings of the people of God, *but yet they sinned.*

(Ex. 17:6)
2

(Ex. 14:22)
(Psalm 77:
16-20; 78:13)

> While the central theme of verse 2 is certainly not baptism, it is of interest to note in this reference to Israel's passing through the Red Sea the *method* by which they were baptized. The New Testament does not stress any particular mode, and baptism we know has no saving value in itself, but the story in Exodus

> and the song memorializing it in Psalms, when taken together with this passage, tell explicitly what happened in what Paul calls "baptism." We are told the "clouds *poured out* water" and that they passed through the sea on dry land with a wall of congealed water standing on each side of them. Paul says, "our fathers were *under* the cloud, and all passed through the sea, and were all baptized unto Moses in the cloud and in the sea."

In spite of the Israelites' relationship with God and **5** His constant leading, "with many of them God was not **6** well pleased," and these were "over thrown ("strewed," dead) in the wilderness." The sins of the Israelites are specifically named as a warning to us. They were **7-10** idolatry, fornication, unbelief and murmuring.

To him Israel was an outstanding example for all time **11** of God's judgment on sin, a possibility from which no one is excluded. All this was to be a stern reminder to us upon whom "the ends of the world" [ages] are come, a phrase which seemingly suggests that all history should speak to us in this last *(church) age.* This is followed by the warning, "Wherefore, let him that thinketh he stand- **12** eth take heed lest he fall."

But There Is a Way (13-15)

The situation, however, is never hopeless. God has provided an escape from sin and judgment. There is no **13** temptation which is overwhelming. No person can say his temptation is unique or unduly oppressive. God will always provide a way of escape. It is on these grounds then that one should deal with sin and expect victory.

As we learned in chapter 8, some of the Corinthians **14** went at times to the pagan feasts to "sit at meat" with those with whom they had formerly associated, thus placing themselves in a situation where they might fall back into idolatry. Paul is reminding them that they were not above being overtaken again by the same sin

from which they felt with overconfidence they had been freed. He warns them to "flee from idolatry." At this
15 point he appeals to them on the grounds of their self-acclaimed "wisdom." With their wisdom they should be able to *know* that what he is saying is right.

The Communion Feast and Eating
Meat Offered to Idols (16-33)

Paul logically ties together the communion feast and
16 the sacrificial feasts in honor of idols. They surely could not eat at the devil's table one time, and the next time at the Lord's table. Earlier in the chapter he had reminded them how the Israelites at one point in their wilderness
(Num. 25) wanderings had "sat down to eat and drink" with the pagans of Moab and then "rose up to play," committing fornication. The connection is clear. The Corinthians were all too familiar with the pagan rites associated with
(8:10) the pagan temples of their city which could so easily become a snare to them as they sat down with their neighbors to eat with them of their seemingly harmless sacrifices. Communion itself denotes fellowship (the Greek word is *koinonia*) and unity with Christ and
17 fellow-believers. As bread represents many crushed grains made into a whole, so the body of Christ is made up of many individuals. "The cup of blessing which we bless" and the bread which we break represents the blood
(John 6) and body of a living Christ through whom we have life.

Not that idols are anything or that meat sacrificed to them is anything, but association in any way with the
18-20 pagan rites automatically places one in fellowship with devils! One cannot sit at the Lord's table and enjoy *koinonia* there and then rise up and attempt also to experience *koinonia* at the Devil's table. They must not think that they are so strong that they can outwit God
22 who had amply warned them.

72

He continues now in more detail the theme of chapter 8 on eating meat offered to idols. Paul has a jealous regard for another's conscience because of that person's ultimate spiritual welfare. The Christian's liberty or personal rights are somewhat hedged in by the other man's conscience. Mere giving of thanks, though it may sanctify the food, still does not give one license to **30** eat it, that is, if this act becomes a hindrance to those who have a conscience against it.

When invited to a pagan home, it is all right to go, and as long as nothing is said about the meat, it is wisest **27** to eat it without asking any questions as to whether or not it may have been sacrificial meat.

However, if someone informs you that it had been **28** offered to idols, then you must refrain from eating it for **(See discus-** the sake of the conscience of the one sitting by. **sion on Ch. 8)**

At this point Paul introduces a new level of consideration. Earlier he was concerned about causing a man to **31** stumble because of an unwise act. Now he states a principle that might well be placed alongside the Golden Rule: "Whether therefore ye eat, or drink, or whatsoever ye do, do all to the glory of God." Keeping this in mind the Corinthians were to be interested in the welfare of all men—Jews, Gentiles, and fellow-Christians—that all **32** might be won for Christ and thus bring Him ultimate glory.

Paul's guiding principle was not to seek his own advantage but that which would profit many—*that they* **33** *might be saved*. This was altruism of a very high order. In verse 24 he had said, "Let no man seek his own, but every man another's." The word "wealth" is not found in the original Greek. Paul is simply saying let each seek the other's *welfare*.

CHAPTER XI

GOD'S ORDER IN CREATION SYMBOLIZED IN WOMEN'S VEILING   CHRIST'S ACT OF REDEMPTION SYMBOLIZED IN THE BREAD AND CUP

Introductory Comments—How We Understand Paul's Teaching

The paucity of scholarly studies on the women's veiling is certainly apparent. This is difficult to understand in view of the fact that there is no evidence that the teaching of Paul on this point can be easily set aside as being outside the range of apostolic tradition. The disproportionate space used in this commentary for this section of Paul's letter we feel is therefore justified.

Because of the wide variation of views on the use of the veiling, special attention is being given first to the problem of interpretation. The writer belongs to a faith that has included the women's veiling in its historic practices and therefore has a deep appreciation for this teaching. With this kind of background, however, one may easily be charged for reading into this Scripture what is not there, a process of interpretation sometimes referred to as *isegesis.* This is not our purpose, to be sure, but rather to engage in faithful *exegesis,* trying to determine what the Scripture actually teaches and how this applies today.

Generalize or Particularize?

In Paul's introduction to this letter he moved quickly, as we have seen, from "the church of God which is at Corinth," to "all that in every place call upon the name of Jesus Christ," making clear the relationship of that part of his teaching meant for a particular time and place and that which has universal application. The wider implications

74

of his writings are immediately seen.

We are convinced that an honest appraisal of the entire Epistle will reveal the universal character of Paul's teachings. Because of the crucial importance of this concept for our immediate consideration in this chapter, we want to call attention briefly to the "universals" of the Epistle.

Universals of I Corinthians

Chapter 1 – Sainthood is a universal concept. Christ's relation to the believer is universal. Church divisions are a universal problem.

Chapter 2 – Preaching "Christ crucified" represents the church's universal method and message. Likewise, the concept of the "natural man" versus the "spiritual man" did not apply to only one Greek city, 55 A.D.

Chapter 3 – Church building is a universal task. All men will be held accountable.

Chapter 4 – Ministers, as managers of God's truth, serve a universal role. Paul also writes: "Be ye followers of me . . . as I teach *everywhere* in *every* church."

Chapter 5 – Universally, not only at Corinth, the church must exercise discipline against immoral members.

Chapter 6 – Saints judging the world, the unrighteous being excluded from the kingdom of God, the saints being raised bodily in the resurrection, our bodies being temples of the Holy Ghost—all of these are universal teachings applying to all men.

Chapter 7 – Proper marriage relations are universally essential. Note the expressions: "any man," "every man," "he that is married," "they that weep," etc., and the statement, "And so I ordain in *all the churches.*"

Chapter 8 – The doctrine of the Godhead and the matter of problems of conscience are not Corinthian concerns only—they have universal application.

Chapter 9 – Of universal concern are the rights and responsibilities of the ministry.

Chapter 10 – Sin, temptation, Christian victory, the communion, and conscience, are all universals.

Chapter 11 – The divine order of creation is a universal. The terms "every man," "every woman," "man and woman" are generic terms. Hair is a universal covering of human heads; it was not only a Corinthian characteristic. Angels bear a universal relationship to Christian believers. Communion is universally observed.

Chapter 12 – God, Jesus Christ, the Holy Spirit, gifts of the Spirit, the church as a body, are all universal concepts and doctrines.

Chapter 13 – Love is a universal grace. This chapter remains the classic psalm of love, with world-wide significance for all time.

Chapter 14 – Church-building is a universal task. Paul refers to his teachings as applying "in all the churches of the saints." His teachings, he says, are the "commandments of the Lord."

Chapter 15 – The resurrection will include all men. Not only the Corinthians will be raised in the Great Resurrection.

Chapter 16 – Quoted frequently as applying universally are the words: "Watch ye, stand fast in the faith, quit you like men, be strong." The Epistle closes with a universal warning: "If *any man* love not the Lord Jesus Christ, let him be Anathema [accursed] Maranatha [Jesus is coming!] "

The Woman's Veiling (2-16)

The Passage Quoted (From the King James translation)

2 Now I praise you, brethren, that ye remember me in all things, and keep the ordinances, as I delivered them to you.

3 But I would have you know, that the head of every man is Christ; and the head of the woman is the man; and the head of Christ is God.

4 Every man praying or prophesying, having his head covered, dishonoureth his head.

5 But every woman that prayeth or prophesieth with her head uncovered dishonoureth her head: for that is even all one as if she were shaven.

6 For if the woman be not covered, let her also be shorn:

but if it be a shame for a woman to be shorn or shaven, let her be covered.

For a man indeed ought not to cover his head, **7** forasmuch as he is the image and glory of God: but the woman is the glory of the man.

For the man is not of the woman; but the woman of the **8** man.

Neither was the man created for the woman; but the **9** woman for the man.

For this cause ought the woman to have power on her **10** head because of the angels.

Nevertheless neither is the man without the woman, **11** neither the woman without the man, in the Lord.

For as the woman is of the man, even so is the man also **12** by the woman; but all things of God.

Judge in yourselves: is it comely that a woman pray **13** unto God uncovered?

Doth not even nature itself teach you, that if a man have **14** long hair, it is a shame unto him?

But if a woman have long hair, it is a glory to her: for **15** her hair is given her for a covering.

But if any man seem to be contentious, we have no such **16** custom, neither the churches of God.

The Passage Quoted (From the Goodspeed translation)

I appreciate you always remembering me, and your **2** standing by the things I passed on to you, just as you received them. But I want you to understand that Christ **3** is the head of every man, while a woman's head is her husband, and Christ's head is God. Any man who offers **4** prayer or explains the will of God with anything on his

5 head disgraces his head, and any woman who offers prayer or explains the will of God bareheaded disgraces her head, for it is just as though she had her head shaved.
6 For if a woman will not wear a veil, let her cut off her hair too. But if it is a disgrace for a woman to have her hair cut off or her head shaved, let her wear a veil. For a
7 man ought not to wear anything on his head, for he is the image of God and reflects his glory; while woman is
8 the reflection of man's glory. For man was not made from woman, but woman was made from man, and man
9 was not created for woman, but woman was for man.
10 That is why she ought to wear upon her head something to symbolize her subjection, out of respect to the angels,
11 if to nobody else. But in union with the Lord, woman is not independent of man nor man of woman. For just as
12 woman was made from man, man is born of woman, and both like everything else really come from God. Judge
13 for yourselves. Is it proper for a woman to offer prayer
14 to God with nothing on her head? Does not nature itself teach you that for a man to wear his hair long is degrading,
15 but a woman's long hair is her pride? For her hair is
16 given her as a covering. But if anyone is disposed to be contentious about it, I for my part recognize no other practice in worship than this, and neither do the churches of God.

How Chapter 11 Has Been Interpreted

There are essentially five different ways in which students of the Bible have looked at this passage:

1. *A Local Problem* – Paul was establishing regulations to correct a local problem in the Corinthian church.
2. *Of Passing Significance* – Paul was dealing with a purely cultural problem that had only passing significance.
3. *Only for the Assembly* – Paul was simply establishing some rules for public worship to help correct local

disorders. Women were to wear the veiling in public worship. Some insist, too, that Paul's rules applied only to married women.

4. *Only for Communion* – Since the latter part of the chapter deals with the communion service, Paul was saying that women should be veiled during holy communion.

5. *A Universal Teaching* – Paul was establishing a regulation for all Christians, memorializing for all time the divine order of headship, the women's veiling being a constant reminder of this relationship.

The whole logic of what Paul was saying earlier, as already indicated, seems definitely to favor the fifth approach. It is very clear from the context that Paul is dealing here with more than a cultural or ethnic custom in a city of Asia Minor, 55 A.D. While it is true that Paul is dealing with some specific problems of that period, the malpractice does not invalidate the tradition he was trying to establish. For example, Paul was trying to correct some bad practices associated with the communion, yet no one would argue that communion was to be observed only by the Corinthian church for that particular period. One can then rightfully raise the question as to how one can generalize the latter part of the chapter, giving it universal application for all churches for all time, and then particularize the first part, limiting it to a particular church for a particular period. Both the veiling and communion are identified in the first verse as *traditions to keep.*

Note how chapter eleven would have read, had it applied only to the church at Corinth:

But I would have you *Corinthians* know that the head of every *Corinthian* man is Christ; and the head of every *Corinthian* woman is the *Corinthian* man. And the head of Christ, for *Corinthians*, is God.

Every *Corinthian* man praying or prophesying having his head covered, dishonoureth his head.

But every *Corinthian* woman that prayeth or prophesieth with her head uncovered dishonoureth her head, etc.

Or one might introduce the time element, saying it applied only to the time when Paul wrote these words. Then it would have read:

> Every man praying or prophesying during the period *from A.D. 50 to A.D. 100* having his head veiled, dishonoureth his head, etc.

The very structure of the passage implies too that it was not written just to remedy a local situation. In chapter seven where Paul is writing about marriage he refers to the expediency of the "present distress." If the problem he was seeking to remedy here had been purely local, the passage would probably have read something like this:

> For the *present time* I would have you women to be veiled and you men to remain unveiled, so that your new-found freedom in Christ be not misunderstood. I do not want you brethren at Corinth to disregard your Corinthian husband-wife mores, so that through this the outside public will stumble at what they consider impropriety.

But there is nothing in the wording that gives any indication of such a localized interpretation, for a specific place, or a specific time or a specific situation.

In all the other instances of dealing with the various problems and disorders, such as immorality in chapter 5, the matter of litigation in chapter 6, the marital problems in chapter 7, or the problem of eating meat offered to idols in chapters 8 and 10, there were abiding principles which he was establishing. What then are the abiding principles emerging from chapter 11 if the veiling has significance beyond that of the immediate situation? Since Paul refers to God's creative order and man's relationship to Christ in God, there seems to be, in fact, a very definite principle which he is attempting to memorialize here through this symbol.

80

Social Aspect—The Matter of Propriety—
The Universality of the Practice

There is a basic social significance to the wearing of the veiling, which lies deeper than any local or ethnic aspect. There seems to have been a general custom among all ancient peoples that women should be veiled in the presence of men. This custom has been carried down through these many centuries so that even in modern times this is still a recognized custom in certain Eastern countries. What Paul was saying, essentially, is that Christian women should not take license in their new-found freedom in Christ to disregard a custom that had had such a respected origin, particularly when they were "praying or prophesying." Such action would most certainly nullify their witness in the eyes of the public.

The Old Testament makes it clear that it was both a Hebrew and a Chaldean custom. Rebekah, in far away Chaldea, on seeing men approaching in the field where she was walking, "took a veil and covered herself." This story predated by many years, the Mosaic period. But it was also part of the Law itself. A woman suspected of adultery was ordered to be stripped of her veil as a sign of her impropriety. **(Gen. 24:65)** **(Num. 5:18)**

Likewise the prophets speak of this. Isaiah, in describing the downfall of the "virgin daughter of Babylon," wrote:

> Come down, and sit in the dust, O virgin daughter of Babylon . . . O daughter of the Chaldeans: for thou shalt no more be called tender and delicate. Take the millstones and grind meal: *uncover thy locks,* make bare the leg, uncover the thigh . . .
> Thy nakedness shall be uncovered, yea thy shame shall be seen. I will take vengeance, and I will not meet thee as a man.

(Isa. 47:1-3)

It is important to note here the apparent step-by-step regression toward shamelessness, in which the first step

81

was *unveiling the head.* Clarke shows that the unveiled head was also a sign of unchastity among the Greeks. He comments on I Corinthians: "Propriety and decency of conduct are the points which the apostle seems to have more especially in view." He says that a woman in those ancient times appearing without a veil "would be considered a disgrace to her husband, suspected to be not very sound in her morals." A number of other commentators agree on this explanation. Shepard has this comment to give on the social situation in Corinth:

> Some of the Christian women had fallen into the error of disregarding the Christian tradition Paul had given them, based on the Genesis order of creation, and were praying and prophesying or speaking in the public assemblies of the church without using the veil, which was the symbol of their correct subordination in the worship service. This was proving a scandal and obstruction to the progress of the cause, because among the Greeks only the lewd women (heterae), who were very numerous in Corinth, *went about the streets unveiled.* (Italics added.) Paul would not have the Christian women, thus, by disregarding the custom of the veiling, to place themselves in a class with the courtesans or lewd women (Shepard, p. 241).

While in one sense Shepard seems to limit the use of the veiling to the worship service, he speaks at the same time of the lewd women who "went about the streets unveiled." The indication is that if the Christian women wore the veiling only in the public assemblies and went about the streets unveiled, they would still be classed with the "heterae."

Lenski, in defending the adoption of this national custom on the basis of a deeper origin, says,

> Paul is not introducing into these national customs

something that is foreign and unjustifiable but is unveiling to Christians the full and true significance of these customs which non-Christians grasped or felt only partially because the glory of the true God was hidden from them.

Jamieson, et. al., in discussing the new-found freedom of the Christian women at Corinth wrote:

The Corinthian women on the ground of the abolition of distinction of sexes in Christ, claimed equality with the male sex, and overstepping the bounds of propriety, came forward to pray and prophesy without the customary headcovering of females. The Gospel doubtless did raise women from the degradation in which they had been sunk, especially in the East. Yet, whilst on a level with males as to the offer of, and standing in grace (Gal. 3:28), their subjection in point of order, modesty, and seemliness is to be maintained.

It is clear, too, that it was not a symbol for married women only. The same commentators refer to it as an "emblem of maiden modesty before men (Gen. 24:65) *and* conjugal chastity" (Gen. 20:16). Smith says simply, "The veil was the mark of a modest woman . . . The regulation was approved by the Christian church and was imposed on Gentile communities; and thus the action of those Corinthian women was a violation of canonical order."

Because of the social significance of the veiling *on the streets* in Corinth it seems well established then that the veiling was more than a symbol to be worn by married women in public worship. Jamieson, et. al., referring to Paul's later command for women to keep silence, supports the broader use: "Even those women endowed with prophecy were designed to exercise their gift rather *in other times and places than the public congregation."* (Italics added.)

Many of those who practice the wearing of the veiling in our time would agree that the veiling serves a wider purpose than merely as a *sanctuary* veil. In its broadest significance it is a socio-religious symbol founded on the order of creation and on the distinction of the sexes, as a mark of chastity and propriety. Thus, while one might say that the modern context is totally different from that of ancient Corinth, meaning, of course, that the significance of the veil would be different, this would be making a quick unwarranted assumption about its current value without any regard to its historic implications for society as a whole.

The point is that the present boldness and freedom of the sexes and laxity in sexual morality must have some underlying causes which must be accounted for in some manner. One needs only to reflect on the history of the "liberation" of the female sex in the past fifty years to note the same moral regression spoken of by Isaiah. The uncovering of the locks and cutting of the hair of the roaring twenties moved women rapidly in a few decades to the "baring of the leg" and the "uncovering of the thigh."

Thus, however one may reason, the social significance of I Corinthians cannot be discounted. Life cannot be separated from worship. The dimensions of the social relationship of the sexes certainly reach out far beyond the sanctuary, and therefore any kind of interpretation that limits the meaning of the veil to that of a quaint little religious symbol to be worn by a small group of culturally-bound women during worship service would be doing violence to the whole concept of the Christian ethic of *religion-in-life*. To summarize, one sees in the veiling a meaning which has roots in the social and spiritual fabric of our social order.

The matter of universal observance in terms of history is also clear. The oldest organized religion, Catholicism, has had this as a perpetual practice in the sanctuary. For many centuries this custom has been observed generally throughout Christendom. And even in our day it is still a custom in public assemblies of whatever sort, and particularly in church assemblies, for men to remain uncovered and women (if they choose) to be covered. This of course is not actually what Paul was teaching in this chapter. He was not talking about rules of etiquette. He is also not talking about men removing their protection headgear. But we simply point this out to show that we are dealing here with a social custom of long standing. And interestingly, there are many women of the various denominations who to this day, out of some kind of compulsion, wear *some kind* of covering (not necessarily a protection covering) in worship services, while men remain uncovered out of "reverence" for the house of God. Likewise the wedding veil, used almost universally by Christian groups who do not observe the veiling tradition of Paul, is an apparent vestige of the original Pauline veil.

Jewish men to this day keep their heads covered with a special prayer cap in the synagogue services, and Paul was also showing, in part, the impropriety of this practice in his restatement of the veiling doctrine, which was apparently observed at that time in all the Christian churches.

The use of religious symbols is certainly not foreign to any culture. In Christendom there are the dangling crosses in jewelry, various pins and insignia, and the elaborate symbolism in art and architecture. The importance of biblical symbols is that they are given under the inspiration of the Holy Spirit and therefore have divine sanction. With their observance comes a blessing

85

for obedience. While human reason may not be able to explain the full significance of the divine symbols, neither can anyone explain fully the meaning of man-devised symbols. It would be difficult to explain, for **(Judges 16:19)** example, how long hair, as in the case of Sampson, could add physical strength, but the fact remains God recognized this through Sampson's vows as a mark of His presence.

Jesus condemned the Pharisees for setting aside the commandments of God for the traditions of men. In our culture many Christians have strangely set aside the biblical symbol of the veil for the man-created symbol of the *wedding ring* to attempt to show the relationship of man and woman. The first is said to have lost its meaning, yet the second is said to have deep significance!

Verse by Verse Comments on I Corinthians 11

Traditions to Keep (1-2)

1 "Be ye followers of me, even as I also am of Christ," comes as a fitting conclusion to chapter 10 and a good introduction to chapter 11. Paul had just said that he always kept others in mind, not seeking his own "profit." In this respect he wanted them to be followers or imitators of him, yet not of himself but of Christ. He hopes his example will cause them to imitate Christ. Paul was to be followed as an imitator and as a teacher of **(14:37)** Christ's doctrines. Later he says, "If any man think himself to be a prophet or spiritual, let him acknowledge that the things that I write unto you are the commandments of the Lord." One writer, commenting on Paul's relationship to Christ, says that instead of being the "creator" or the "corrupter" of the Christianity of Christ, as some schools of criticism have boldly charged, "he is on the contrary the greatest interpreter of Christ and true Christianity."

This chapter more properly begins with verse 2. In his 2 tactful way Paul approaches the Corinthians on two traditions which he praised them for keeping. It seems clear that they had been practicing these on the basis of his previous teaching, and he was now giving the foundational truth underlying them. There is little value in observing meaningless ritual. The ready obedience of this church in the face of some definite shortcomings otherwise, is most noteworthy. Jamieson, et. al., commenting on "traditions to keep," note that it is difficult "to know what is a genuine apostolic tradition intended for all ages. Any [tradition] that can be proved to be such [a genuine apostolic tradition] ought to be observed; any that cannot ought to be rejected. *Those preserved in the written word alone can be proved to be such.*" (Italics added.)

The matter of "externals" has been a frequent subject for controversy, some insisting they have no place in the Christian life. There is a possibility, of course, of overemphasizing them to the neglect of the inner life. But here we have at least two examples of externals which were delivered to be observed. Morris points out that the article [the] suggests "well-known Christian traditions. They were not Paul's own. The teachings had been handed down to Paul, and he passed them on to the converts. The term stresses the derivative nature of the Gospel. It does not originate in the fertile mind of the teacher" (Morris, p. 151). Note Paul's comment in verse two compared with his directive in his later letter to the Thessalonians: "Therefore, brethren, stand fast, **(II Thess. 2:15)** and hold the traditions which ye have been taught, whether by word, or our epistle." The seriousness of not following the traditions is also underscored in the chapter following: "Now we command you, brethren, in **(II Thess. 3:6)** the name of our Lord Jesus Christ, that ye withdraw yourselves from every brother that walketh disorderly, and not after the tradition which he received of us." These traditions were to be kept whether oral or written. The modern movement of the church to drop the wearing of the veiling started in a small degree but has gone beyond the point of return. Churches do not generally return to traditions once lost (Davis). For that reason it is of utmost importance to hold fast to those which are clearly of divine origin.

The Creative Order of Headship; the Role of the Sexes (3, 8, 9, 11, 12)

3   The matter of headship in the divine order of creation is clearly spelled out: "The head of every man is Christ, and the head of the woman is the man, and the head of Christ is God." While there are some minor differences of interpretation among expositors as to the exact meaning of this headship scheme, that there is some intended hierarchical order cannot be disputed. The whole context of the Scriptures supports this, and this idea definitely forms the key to the interpretation of the first part of chapter 11. Schematically this order may be shown as follows:

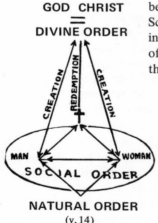

God and Christ are equal, yet there is an order of priority.

Man and woman are equal in Christ, yet there is an order of priority.

Note particularly the relation of this teaching to the "natural order" and the social order, the latter of which has already been discussed. More will be said later about the order of nature.

Modern crusades for the equality of the sexes ignore the basic elements of God's creative order. Male and female are neither equal nor unequal, but were made to complement each other—physically, socially, and spiritually—a truth which many fail to grasp. "Either sex alone is half itself . . . each fulfills defect in each, and always thought in thought, purpose in purpose, will in will they grow . . . the two-celled beat beating with one full stroke, life" (Tennyson). "By divine appointment the woman is rightly subordinate but not wrongly enslaved to man" (Shepard). Paul "is not arguing for anything other than a partnership (cf. verse 11), though a partnership in which the man is the head of his household" (Morris). "The subordination itself (of recognizing her head) has its foundations planted deep in man's *principatus* or lordship by creation . . . The woman therefore is *morally bound* to exhibit . . . the public token of her constitutional subjection to man" (Cook).

Paul goes back to the creation account to explain the basis for his argument. The woman being "of man" refers to the Genesis story where we read of Eve's being **(Gen. 2: 21-23)** made from a rib taken from Adam's side. That is also the source of the statement that the man was not created for the woman but the woman for the man. God had said that "It is not good that the man should be **(Gen. 2:18)** alone: I will make him an help meet (suitable) for him." "Neither in her origin, nor in the purpose for which she was created can the woman claim priority, or even equality" (Morris).

But just so the man cannot claim superiority over the

woman or demand her subordination to him. For although he was first in the order of creation, he is now, through the process of birth, also "of the woman." Their partnership under God is expressed in Paul's final statement that "all things are of God." Peter, discussing the marriage relationship refers to the husband and wife **(I Pet. 3:7)** as being "heirs together of the grace of life." Failure to recognize God's divine order will only result in utter chaos to society. There will be a return to the law of the jungle or to barnyard ethics as men violate this order and **(Rom. 1:** adopt such ideas as "total equality" of the sexes, **24-29)** "unisex," or homosexuality.

The Veiling (4-7, 10, 13-16)

It must be remembered that Paul is not establishing two new practices in chapter 11 (veiling and communion). He is only meeting some of the problems that arose in connection with the practice of both, which as was already pointed out, were being observed in some fashion in all the churches.

4 Looking specifically at the verses which deal with the veiling we learn that the woman is to be veiled during those times she is praying or "prophesying" (explaining the will of God—Goodspeed), and that the man is not to be veiled. To violate this simple code is to dishonor their mutual head, Christ. The Scripture quotation, stated in the meaning of the Greek runs as follows: "Any man praying or prophesying with anything on his head (implying a veiling or special prayer cap (tallith) such as worn by Jewish men) dishonors his head, but any **5** woman praying or prophesying with her head unveiled dishonors her head." This actually ends Paul's declaration on the veiling. What follows in the seven "for clauses" simply supports his basic apostolic directive.

The significance of a woman "praying or prophesying" with her head covered is that in those most important moments when she is attempting to speak to God in behalf of men or to men in behalf of God, she needs to show her subjection to the divinely-arranged order of headship. "In putting away the veil she puts away the badge of her subjection to man, which is her true 'honor'; for through him it connects her with Christ the head of the man" (Jamieson, et. al.). Cook states that woman is veiled in deference to man her visible head, whereas man's head, Christ, is not visible. Robertson refers to the angels who covered their faces in the presence of **(Isa. 6:2)** God. The Wesleyan Bible Commentary notes that women in the presence of God, Christ, angels and men "should be careful to do nothing indecent or irregular" [page 161].

Very directly the text suggests that she may as well **6** be shorn or shaven if she is not veiled, to give public evidence of her impropriety. This was the identifying mark of those whom society had labelled as lewd. The command, "let her be shorn" suggests the custom of the times to impose this mark of identification upon a disgraced person. "Let her be veiled," is the answer to this unnecessary and grossly misfitting procedure of being shorn—that is for those who were Christians, and hence considered morally upright. In no case should they be mistaken for the *heterae.*

Those who have argued that a woman's hair is given for a covering, as stated in verse 15, ignore the fact that another Greek word is used there for covering. The word used denotes a natural covering that envelops the head, but not a veiling. This kind of interpretation also ignores the simple logic of the preceding verses. For if the hair is the only covering mentioned in I Corinthians 11, then if she be not covered (hair removed), how can she *also* be shorn? The hair cannot be removed twice!

There is still a further incongruity. Those who insist

that the veil should be used in public worship only, need to recognize that the *hair* cannot be laid aside at leisure. Yet the two are shown in this passage as inseparable. Hair and the veiling cannot *both* be put on in worship and both removed on the street. The veiling-and-long-hair symbol does not represent an intermittent God-Christ-man relationship, but a continuing experience. "Let her be veiled" means by its grammatic structure, "Let her *continue* to be veiled." Similarly, the *heterae* would continue to be shaved and shorn to identify them as long as they remained in the harlot class. Paul's teaching, in short, is tied in with the theme of long-hair-veiled for women and short-hair-unveiled for men. Davis, who has made a detailed exegetical study of I Corinthians 11, says, "It is no less a disgrace to pray unveiled out of the church than in it." Paul is saying that "wherever and whenever it is proper . . . to pray or to prophesy, the difference of sex should be marked as I indicate" (Lenski). And since prophesying means, "explaining the will of God," "instructing," "encouraging," "exhorting," "edifying," "comforting," who would begin to suggest that all of these functions or ministries should be carried on only in the public assembly?

7   Since the man is not to be covered while praying or prophesying (if the hair serves as a covering), this would hardly suggest then that he is to be shaved every time he prays or prophesies. Without attempting to be facetious it would seem evident, however, that according to the teachings of some, to carry out correctly the teachings of I Corinthians both men and women would need to wear wigs, which could then be put on and off readily for church or street.

10   A very interesting reason for the wearing of the veil is suggested now when Paul says, "For this cause ought the woman to have power (authority) on her head because

of the angels." The full significance of this may not be understood, but the fact that these heavenly messengers are drawn into the picture at this point underscores the importance of this apostolic tradition. It may have reference to those guardian angels who surround every believer, and in this light the veil would serve as a badge or sign that the praying or prophesying woman is in full obedience. Angels are shown in the Bible as those heavenly beings who are always in full subjection to God. To such this would have special meaning.

Paul now shifts to an appeal to "natural law" or to **13-15** the order of nature, explaining his position through some of the "for" clauses. He asks, Doesn't your own sense of propriety tell you that it is not becoming "or suitable to female modesty" (Benson) for "a woman to pray to God unveiled"? (ABUV, Broadus, et. al.). "Doesn't even nature itself teach you that it is a shame for a man to have long hair but a glory for a woman? By nature woman is endowed with a symbol of modesty . . . The veil is merely the artificial continuation of her natural [God-given gift of] hair" (Marcus Dods, *The Expositors Bible,* p. 253). "In the sculptures of the catacombs the (Christian) women have a close-fitting head-dress while the men have the short hair" (Vincent, *Word Studies*). "Is it comely?" means, "Do you think it right and proper for a woman to pray to God bare-headed?" (Phillips). "Is it becoming that a woman pray to God unveiled?" (ABUV, Broadus, et. al.).

Long hair, says Paul, is a shame to a man. This has not been universally the case in all cultures. Even in ancient Greece, particularly among the Spartans and among some of the philosophers long hair on men was not uncommon. In more modern times the male American Indian has worn long hair in braids. Morris says, however, that "generally speaking what Paul says held among mankind. Exceptions were local and temporary." The fact that Nazarites in Hebrew history grew long hair under a vow indicates that short hair was the general practice. Whatever exceptions have occurred in the various cultures does not detract from Paul's generalization based presumably on basic ancient culture connotations.

It should be noted, however, that I Corinthians 11 is not a study of coiffures, nor does it stipulate the exact length of a man's or a woman's hair. How long, for example, must a man's hair be to be a shame, or how short a woman's hair to be a shame? What Paul is talking about is a discernible difference between the sexes which even nature and respectability teach. Paul obviously intends that women's hair should be of natural length.

14, 15 "Is not the male sex, having short hair, by nature unveiled, and the female, having long hair, by nature veiled? If luxuriant tresses are a glory to a woman because they are given her as nature's veil, surely the textile fabric also, the moral badge of subordination is equally becoming to her, inasmuch as it indicates her perception of harmony between what is physical and what is ethical in God's order of things" (Cook, 322). *Paribolaion* is used in verse 15 to signify the hair as a mantle enveloping her head. The word *katakalupto* is the word for covering used in verses 4, 5, 6, 7 and, as stated above, means "veil." "Kata" (down) suggests a veil hanging down, completely covering the head.

16 Paul says that if any man contests his teachings, he wants it clearly understood that there is "no such custom" anywhere among the churches as going unveiled. The construction here seems to make this the only logical interpretation. It would hardly be plausible, after all of his detailed instructions to conclude by saying that if any man is contentious about the use of the veiling, they should simply drop the custom.

While some commentators and Bible scholars have **17** reasoned that the veiling is only for the public assembly, the use of the words, "come together," and "come together in the church" in verses 17 and 18 in the introduction to Paul's instructions on the communion service, indicate that this particular sacrament was to be practiced in the assembly and not in public. The same expression occurs in chapter 5, where he deals with the gathered group engaged in the administration of church discipline. If both traditions, the veiling and communion, were meant for the gathered group alone, this statement would most likely have occurred at the beginning of the chapter in some such manner as: "Now I praise you brethren, that ye remember me in all things and keep the ordinances *when ye are come together.*"

The Matter of Attitudes

In concluding this rather lengthy exposition on the veiling a word should be said on the matter of attitudes. On a doctrine that has such a wide variation of interpretation if one is not careful, he can easily get "puffed up" against those who make a different application. Certainly the wearing or non-wearing of the veiling should not result in a spirit of pride or arrogance with persons taking a judgmental attitude toward those who may see this in a different light, particularly in terms of *how* it should be observed. Our method of application should not be the means of causing a weak member to stumble, recalling the earlier discussions in chapters 8 and 10. But if there is any doubt as to whether or not the veiling should be worn at all, it would seem that the proper thing to do would be "to give God the benefit of the doubt." It is perhaps not so much a matter as to *what kind* of veiling should be worn or *when,* or *where,* as to *whether* some form of veiling is worn at all at any time. In quibbling over the matter of where or when or what kind there is always a possibility of ending up wearing none.

Motives are important. Is the church really seeking the will of God today in such matters, or is it a matter of leaving it to individual choice on the basis of personal reason or expediency? By failing to deal with any teaching in an open manner there is a possibility of losing it by default.

The writer's personal feeling is that the little prayer caps worn today by many plain sects represent a noble attempt to express an historic biblical tradition. Yet, among those who observe it, the modern version of the veiling has become so abbreviated in many instances that it no longer begins to *cover* the head, which was the original intent of the veiling. But even in these instances it might be better to exercise the word of encouragement than to use ridicule. Perhaps the more traditional opaque style worn by sisters of certain believers' groups in Latin America and India is more scriptural in this respect, since it does cover the head (or hair) far more adequately. This style could be adopted by the North American and European Christian women. Such a veiling, somewhat similar to the simpler types of wedding veils worn today, would serve a double purpose. It would give a certain dignity wherever she is seen and would also help to serve as a mark of identity. And thus, wherever she would go, when the occasion arose to pray or to "explain the will of God" (Goodspeed) to anyone, she would have her badge of authority to do it. It would serve further as a symbol of chastity in a day when many immodest women are walking the streets of our cities. This would imply, of course, that the other part of her apparel would be consistent with the veiling. A veil of this sort would by no means diminish, but rather enhance, a woman's beauty and femininity and at the same time help to eliminate all her constant worrying about hairdos and the time and expenditure involved in trying to look attractive. At the same time there would be a resulting peace and happiness in knowing that she is in the will of God, obedient to the teachings of the Bible which were designed by God in the first place, not for restraint but for her ultimate good.

To argue that such a requirement is totally unrealistic in our time is ridiculous in light of the many crazy styles and patterns exhibited in our contemporary culture. A casual walk down any street today will help anyone to understand what grotesque demands Dame Fashion is making. It would seem that the errors which had crept into Corinthian practices on both the veil and communion were probably no worse than modern errors that have crept in. God's blessing is always on those who seek His will and who in finding that will, attempt to explain it to others, whether in the home, church, or in the market place.

The Communion (Lord's Supper), Another Church Tradition (17-34)

This is the first place in the New Testament writings where we are informed on the institution of the Lord's Supper. The Gospels had not yet been written. For that reason it was important to have the churches correctly informed as to the significance of the event as well as to give instructions on its proper observance.

Paul notes that he had received this instruction "of the Lord." Whether he had received a special revelation on this as he had on some other occasions or whether he received it through oral tradition from Luke and others is not certain. The means is not important if divine revelation is our basic premise for accepting any Scrip-

23
(Acts 18:9;
22:18; 23:11;
27:23-25;
Gal. 1:12; 2:2;
II Cor. 12:7)

97

ture. The likelihood here according to most commentators is that Paul had received these instructions from the Lord through others.

As in the case of the veiling, they had already received earlier instructions from him, and he was not merely attempting to correct some bad practices that had developed in the observance of the Lord's supper.

17-22 The problem of eating and feasting was apparently a Corinthian weakness, yet hardly more so than today. If Paul were here today, he would no doubt have to say much in the same manner as he did to the Corinthians, When you are come together, this is not merely to eat—have you not houses to eat in? Our Lord himself would no doubt upset many dinner tables in modern church houses as he upset the tables of the money changers in the temple. To return to the Corinthian setting, it appears that the idea of feasting, always associated with the idol worship, was simply translated into a kind of Christian banquet in connection with the Lord's supper. Paul was trying to correct their excesses. They were eating a full meal instead of observing a token feast. Paul is not condemning the "feasts of charity"

(Jude 12) apparently observed by the Early Church in connection with the regular communion, which actually was an orderly meal. What was happening was a kind of travesty on the very idea of *koinonia* or fellowship, for it seems that each one ate *before his neighbor* his own provision in a greedy manner whether or not his brother had anything. Some therefore who were poor went away

20, 21 hungry while others ate and drank in excess.

22 In a series of rhetorical questions he lays open their "heresies." He could not praise them for such conduct

(2) although he did praise them for keeping the tradition of the Lord's supper. The answers are clear. Home is the place to eat, not the church. By eating in front of the poor who have tiny lunches or nothing you are shaming them and through this gesture of unbrotherliness despising all the church stands for.

The story which follows in the next number of verses is familiar to all Christians who have participated in the communion service. What Paul writes is very similar to the later writings of the four Evangelists.

> The Lord Jesus the same night in which he was betrayed took bread: and when he had given thanks he brake it, and said, Take eat: this is my body which is broken for you: this do in remembrance of me. After the same manner also he took the cup, when he had supped, saying, This cup is the New Testament in my blood: this do ye, as oft as ye drink it, in remembrance of me.

23-25

Paul's account differs only in some minor details from the story in the Gospels. Apparently he spells out more definitely the meaning of Christ's words as quoted in Matthew and Luke where he speaks of not eating or drinking anymore "until the kingdom of God shall come." Paul's words are:

20

(Lu. 22:16-18)

> For as often as ye eat this bread, and drink this cup, ye do show the Lord's death till he come.

The beauty and richness of the commemoration based on the supreme sacrifice of Christ on Calvary can never be over-valued. Certainly no more appropriate symbols could have been selected for the feast that was to memorialize perpetually His death and suffering.

There is no sacramental value in the act of eating the bread and drinking the fruit of the vine as some here taught. Neither can one read into this some kind of special miracle. The bread and the juice do not, for example, become the actual body and blood of Christ. If the bread were in actuality his body, it is certain Jesus did not pluck any flesh from his side and hand it to the disciples when he said to them, "Take, eat: this is my body."

Eating and Drinking Unworthily (27-34)

28 Since communion represents atonement for sin, it must be observed in all seriousness. Every man should examine himself. Sometimes people object to communing with those who they feel are not ready to commune, but the responsibility is a personal one. The communicant is not asked to examine other people. Nevertheless, the church as a body does have a responsibility to cleanse itself of offenders as is clearly shown in I Corinthians 5 where Paul says, "with such an one no not to eat," apparently referring to the communion feast. If there is sin in the participant's life or if he engages in a kind of perverted love feast which is marked with banqueting and excess, all of this calls for examina-

27
29 tion. To eat "unworthily" can lead to serious consequences, since such an one eats and drinks "damnation" to himself, not realizing that the body of believers is the outward expression of Christ's atonement. To lift the hand to receive the sacred emblems is saying in a public way before the congregation—"I am redeemed by the blood of Jesus and made a part of His spiritual body—the church." Hence, the hypocrisy of attempting to celebrate the Lord's supper when one is not right with the Lord.

The unworthy recipient does not immediately draw a curse of God upon himself, but God may chasten him. If he were to judge himself, this chastening would not be necessary. But the Lord who loves His own so much will do everything possible to keep them in His grace.

30 "For this cause"—that is partaking of communion unworthily—many are weak and sickly and some have died. The teaching seems to be that God may bring sickness and even death as part of His chastening, grievous though this may be. It may involve the touching of some innocent person with disease or death—one who

himself is right with the Lord—just to woo the offending brother. Or it may mean that God deals with the offender himself through affliction and death. In any case, instead of speaking of God's wrath by which He singles out those who have partaken of communion unworthily, dealing with them roughly, Paul is saying just the opposite. God, through His marvellous dealings, is disciplining His own children so that they may not be eternally lost.

God does not need to judge those who judge themselves. Some may have been eating and drinking to excess, a practice which alone could lead to sickness and death. Or it may simply mean that if those who are not right with God will deal with their own sins through Christ's atonement, as represented in the communion service, He will not need to bring His hand of chastening or perhaps eventual judgment upon them. This is always the purpose of God's chastening—to save men, not to destroy them. **31, 32**

Whatever the church fails to set in order in reference to these violations, Paul will set in order when he comes to visit them again showing once more the place of leadership in discipline. **33, 34**

CHAPTERS XII, XIII, XIV

THE TRIAD

To best understand Paul's teaching on spiritual gifts one must study the next three chapters as a unit. One must remember, of course, that the original letter had no chapter divisions, so that this triad of chapters was simply one major section of his letter. The accompanying chart shows the relationship of these chapters.

To state it briefly, chapter 12 deals with spiritual gifts

and functions in the body of believers. Chapter 13 shows Christian love as superior to all spiritual gifts and manifestations, while chapter 14 compares the best spiritual gift with the poorest.

Chapter 12 begins, "Now concerning spiritual gifts, brethren, I would not have you ignorant . . ." The word "gifts" is not in the Greek text, so that it would read more correctly in English: "Now concerning *'spirituals,'* or *'spirit-manifestations'* . . ." The purpose of the lengthy discussion on these manifestations is obvious as one reads through this section. They were having problems concerning the exercise of these Spirit-workings, and Paul was writing to them to correct this. They lacked understanding, too, concerning each member's place in the body under the Spirit's pattern of operation.

In explaining the various spirit-manifestations, Paul does not deny their use or importance, but he is trying to tell the puffed up Christians at Corinth, who seemingly were vying with each other to show impressive manifestations of the Spirit, that there needs to be a clear understanding both of the place and function of each member of the body. The fact that one person may have a stronger or more spectacular manifestation of the Spirit's presence in his life is no indication that he is more important or more spiritual. Closing this chapter he simply reminds them that if they were seeking spiritual gifts, they should be sure to seek the best: "Covet earnestly the best gifts." And even if they should have all the manifestations of the Spirit in their life, there was still a "more excellent way." That we find in chapter 13.

Chapter 13, the love chapter, is definitely an attempt to show the importance of the wonderful grace of love over and against any Spirit-manifestation. Even though one could speak with the tongues of men and of angels and had no Christian love, he would simply be a

clanging noise. And could one exercise to perfection
the gifts of prophecy, wisdom, discernment, knowledge,
and faith, and had no love, he would be NOTHING. Paul
describes the marvelous workings of love, as compared
with the workings of the Spirit-manifestations. Essentially it is love that makes the body function properly.

The beginning of chapter 14 ties together all that has
gone before with what follows: "Follow after charity
(Christian love), and desire spiritual gifts ('spirituals'), but
rather that ye may prophesy." He is saying, If you are
so eager to have a Spirit-manifestation, make sure you
have the best. He then shows how prophecy is far
superior to tongues.

In reading Paul's second letter to the Corinthians **(II Cor. 8:7)**
written a few years later, one gathers that they had by
that time grown in their exercise of gifts as well as in
love, the latter of which seemed to have been lacking
earlier. They needed yet, however, to grow in the grace
of giving, of which he had spoken in his first letter.

The following chart should help show the relationship
of the three chapters:

Chapter 12	Chapter 13	Chapter 14
SPIRITUAL GIFTS	**CHRISTIAN LOVE**	**PROPHECY COMPARED WITH TONGUES**
(Something to be desired)	(Love better than gifts)	(The best gift of all)
The greatest TASK is *Edifying.*	The greatest WAY is *Love.*	The greatest METHOD of performing the task is *Prophesying.*
12:31–"Covet earnestly the best gifts."	12:31–"A more excellent way."	14:1–"Desire rather that ye may prophesy."
14:12–"Seek that ye may excel to the ed- ifying of the church."	13:13–"The greatest [grace] is love."	14:5–"Greater is he that prophesies than he that speaketh in tongues."
	14:1–"Follow after charity."	14:9–"I had rather [prophesy]."

*Conclusion: 14:39 – "BUT COVET TO PROPHESY, AND
FORBID NOT TO SPEAK IN TONGUES."*

SPIRIT-MANIFESTATIONS
THE BODY FUNCTIONING AS A UNIT

The Spirit and His Differing Manifestations (1-11)

1   Paul is much concerned that no one be ignorant concerning the manifestations of the Spirit. Strangely, though, with all of his clarity there is still much misunderstanding about "spiritual gifts" after these many centuries. The term *spiritual gifts* itself has been loosely applied to include all of the categories of Spirit-manifestations mentioned in this chapter. As noted already, the word "gifts" does not occur in the original Greek in verse 1. A correct rendering is, "Now concerning 'spirituals' *(pneumatikōn)* I would not have you ignorant." Chapter 12 deals with three categories of Spirit-manifestations, which we will note shortly, none of which, singly, can ever be taken as a measure of one's own spiritual status.

2   Converted as they had recently been from paganism, the Corinthians were reminded how they had worshiped dumb idols. They had been "carried away" or blindly led by the blind leaders who taught them that this was the Way. It is difficult to understand how those who claimed to have such a portion of worldly wisdom could convince themselves that idol worship made sense. But this same kind of contradiction was to be found in the Greek philosophers themselves, who with all of their wisdom, worshiped idols. Philosophy itself is never too rational, and neither is much modern worship with its liturgy and ritual in terms of having meaning or (cf. Ch. 1)   relevance to the individual's inner need. But just as they had been "carried away" once, they were again being carried away ignorantly by their emotional immaturity.

The simple logic of chapters 12 to 14 serves as an impressive answer to their professed wisdom.

It is interesting, too, that though they had once worshiped *dumb* idols which obviously could not speak in *any* tongue, they could quickly move over to the other extreme of having many of their group speak in *tongues,* all in one service.

Paul is saying more than this, however. He says the mere fact they had renounced dumb idols to serve **3** the living Christ showed they were born-again children of God—born of the Spirit—for no man, on his own, would be able to call Jesus, "Lord, but by the Holy Ghost." In other words, he is saying, You are Christians, you are spiritually-minded, so let your manifestations of this be spiritual. Paul then explains in detail the various manifestations of the Spirit.

1. There are different kinds of "gifts" *(charismata)*— **4** "gracious endowments leading to miraculous results" (Clarke).

2. There are different kinds of "administrations" **5** *(diakonia)*—services, aids, and offices in the church.

3. There are different kinds of "operations" **6** *(energemata)*—workings of an unusual order.

All of these relate directly to the list of Spirit-mani- **(8-10)** festations and the list of offices mentioned later in the **(28-30)** chapter. These are listed below. Paul says though there are many kinds of manifestations of the Spirit, it is the same God who works in all persons who are endowed or empowered by the Spirit. To every man is given some manifestation of the Spirit which enables him to be **7** fruitful in his own way in the Christian life. None is for vain show. They are not for the personal gratification of the possessor but for the advantage of all believers. Interestingly, too, these *gifts, services,* and *workings* include ministries to the whole man—to body, soul, and spirit.

105

First List (of Spirit-Manifestations) (8-10)

I. Those dealing with the mind and tongue—"gifts" of communication

8
1. The word of wisdom
2. The word of knowledge

II. Those dealing with the body

9, 10
3. Faith
4. Healing
5. Miracles—*(energemata dunameon)* "supernatural supply of energy" (Shepard); "mighty operations" (Clarke).

"Faith" as used here is an operation of the spirit closely associated with healing and performing of miracles—the kind of faith needed for "mighty operations."

III. Those dealing with the spiritual nature of man

10
6. Prophecy—preaching and predicting—dealing with spiritual communication.
7. Discerning of spirits—determining the true prophets.

Discerning of spirits represents the special gift of being able to detect error, whether the speaker is prophesying or speaking in tongues. The Apostle John **(I John 4:1)** wrote: ". . . try the spirits whether they are of God: because many false prophets are gone out into the world." Predictive prophecy as a special gift was demonstrated in Agabus who foretold a dearth (Acts 11:28), and the binding of Paul and delivering him to the Romans (Acts 21:11). Paul also foretold his own shipwreck on Malta (Acts 27:26). Philip had four daughters who prophesied (Acts 21:9).

10
8. Different kinds of tongues
9. Interpretation of tongues

The expression, "different kinds of tongues" raises the question whether there were different kinds of ecstatic tongues or whether this refers to different kinds

106

of languages, *or* specific languages, as one kind, and ecstatic tongues as another kind. It is significant that whereas there are several named in the New Testament who prophesied, there is no one *named* who spoke in tongues, excepting Paul who said of himself that he thanked God that he spoke with tongues "more than ye all" (I Cor. 14:18).

There have been those who have attempted to parallel the two lists—the gifts with the offices. While the relationship is clear, it appears difficult to insist, however, that "wisdom," for example, in list number one matches "apostles" in list number two, etc. There is, counting both lists together, another category of manifestations of the Spirit which definitely comes in the category of "services" *(diakonia),* the word from which our word deacon is derived. They are:

    10. Helps   **28**

    11. Governments

These services which come into the area of ministration and administration are demonstrated numerous times in the New Testament in such people as Aquila and Priscilla, and Stephanus who are definitely referred to as "helps" or "helpers" (Acts 18:2, 18, 26; I Cor. 16:19; and Romans 16:3).

Second List (Those Manifesting the Spirit) (28-30)

And God hath set some in the church:

    1. apostles (first, time-wise and of importance)

    2. prophets

    3. teachers

    4. miracles (miracle workers)

    5. gifts of healing (those who can heal)

    6. governments (officials)

    7. diversities of tongues (those who speak in tongues)

    8. (interpreters of tongues)

The Body, a Unity With the Different Parts
Working Harmoniously Together (12-26)

There are different figures used in the Bible to describe the church. The church is spoken of in different parts of the New Testament as: a *flock* (John 10), a *field* or crop (I Corinthians 3), a *building* (I Corinthians 3), a *body* (I Corinthians 12), a *bride* (Ephesians 5), a *brotherhood* (various places). Each of these is an apt analogy. Some of the very obvious observations in the analogy of the church with the human body are these:

12   1. The body has many members, but still functions as one body.

14-17   2. One member or part of the body would not make a body.

         3. The various parts do not become rivals. If all were an eye, how could one hear, etc.?

18   4. Just as God has arranged the human body to function through its different members coordinated properly, so he has designed the spiritual body—the church—to work coordinately.

21-24   5. Every member needs the other members. Even the most lowly part of the body is needed, and is even honored by the care we give it.

25   6. The body cannot be divided into parts; they must relate to each other.

26   7. One member's hurt, in the human body, is the hurt of the whole body. One member's success is the success of the whole body.

We are at our best when we are members of a body and also something of value alone. One might apply here the saying, "The strength of the wolf is the pack, and the strength of the pack is the wolf."

There are so many persons in our day who feel they can be good Christians without belonging to any church group. This is self-deception. No one is so self-sufficient that he can operate alone. One often notes that as church interest lags, many such persons become members of some service organization, lodge, or club, betraying the fact that man is made to seek fellowship.

Paul compares the unity of the body of Christ with the unity of the human body, and then shows **12** how the unity of the body of Christ is the result of the "one Spirit." Unity involves a working together of the various parts of the body, which includes in its totality the various races or nationalities and the various social classes, "whether we be Jews or Gentiles, whether we be bond or free." In Christ there is a complete **13, 14** blending together of all men through the same Spirit.

The baptism of the Spirit, a subject of much discussion and sometimes controversy is clearly described as being the initiatory rite into the Christian body. This is the teaching of the New Testament. When an individual chooses to follow Christ, he is accepting Christ, but the baptism of the Spirit is God's acceptance of the individual. The New Testament words for the ongoing experience in the Spirit are "indwelling of the Spirit" and "filled with the Spirit." One does not get baptized for special tasks. Baptism is a one-time experience.

Paul is opposed to schisms, or divisions in the body. **25** The secret of the united group is found in the mutual "care one for another." The sentiments expressed in that beautiful hymn, "Blest Be the Tie That Binds" apply here—"We share our mutual woes, our mutual burdens bear, And often for each other flows, the sympathizing tear." It is this kind of experience which makes a pastor feel that his church must truly be part of the Body of Christ, for there is no other organization that can claim the same inner cohesion. If one member suffers, all **26** suffer; if one member is honored, all rejoice with him. **(Rom. 12:15)** This is the ideal. To the Romans he wrote: "Rejoice with them that do rejoice, and weep with them that weep." It is perhaps a bit easier to weep with those who weep than it is to rejoice with those who have achieved some notable success or victory.

Members in Particular (27-31)

In the church there is a well-designed division of labor. The list here names offices or functions rather than spirit-manifestations. It corresponds, though, roughly with the list in the earlier part of this chapter. In either case, whether manifestations or offices these are not inherited, but assigned by God.

Where room is made for the various offices in the church there is the greatest efficiency and the greatest unity. The unity is achieved through diversity. A basketball team is not made up of all forwards or centers; there is a need for guards. A good team member is not one who plays his own game and tries to make all the baskets, but one who is willing to sacrifice some of his personal glory for the sake of the team. It is evident that the list includes at least one office that represents a passing phase in the history of the church. There are no longer any apostles. Some would include in that list the working of miracles and speaking in tongues as also representing a passing phase. At any rate it is not inferred from this or from any other Scripture that any given church must have the full complement of offices or gifts listed in this chapter. Instead the whole history and spread of the church is involved in this particular verse, where it is stated, "God hath set some in the church,

110

first apostles, secondarily prophets, thirdly teachers, etc."
It is also interesting to observe how low in the scale "governments" is placed. The emphasis on church hierarchical posts and officialdom, although popular in later Christianity, and today, apparently was of low esteem in the early Church. Organization is for smooth functioning of the body, not as an end in itself.

He closes with the thought that one should covet the 31 best gifts—but with all of these there is even a more excellent way.

CHAPTER XIII

CHRISTIAN LOVE

Although chapter divisions did not occur in the original language but were simply added by translators, it is obvious that the material covered by this triad of chapters falls into three distinct subject areas. The love chapter is neatly sandwiched in between the two chapters dealing with spirit-manifestations.

The word "charity" used in the King James translation is a good word, although less understood today in its original meaning. Today we think of it as a gift for benevolent purposes, but the original Greek word was *agape*. This word, incidentally, was scarcely used by the Greeks. They were far more familiar with *eros,* the word for erotic love. The Latin root for charity is *caritat-caritas,* meaning "Christian love." It is also akin to the Greek words, *charis* (grace); *charein* (to rejoice); and *charisma* (gifts or favors). The English word comes from a good word family. The Greek word *agape* used in this

111

passage is recognized as having a special Christian meaning. To translate it then as merely "love," as do all the modern versions, tends to lose its uniqueness. For today this word is used to denote almost any kind of emotional attitude of affection, from the passionate Hollywood "thing" to warm filial love *(phileo)* to genuine Christian love.

The above paragraph was finished 4:20 a.m., Feb. 5, 1971, at the moment of man's third landing on the moon. It occurred to me on this memorable occasion that if the money spent on moonflights were used to help express our Christian love to mankind, we would have a different world. Henry Drummond wrote years ago that the world was "dying for a little bit of love."

A reading of chapter thirteen at this point from any Bible available will take only a few minutes and will be very rewarding. The reader may want to read it in several versions.

* * * * * * *

Without Love, Nothing Counts (1-3)

The superior position of Christian love to spirit-manifestations and to good works of any sort, is emphatically underscored with the unusual construction of the three introductory "though" clauses.

1   Though I can speak in tongues

2   Though I have the gifts of prophecy and knowledge and faith

3   Though I give all my goods to feed the poor

WITHOUT CHRISTIAN LOVE I AM NOTHING, AND NOTHING I DO PROFITS ME!

Christian love is the sole credential to proper living. Seldom does the Scripture come through with more emphasis and probably never with greater eloquence

112

than in I Corinthians 13. And happily so, for there must be no crude way of suggesting that we need love! The call for charity itself must exhibit what the very next verse speaks of—kindness.

Good human relations, the greatest concern of this century, are commonly said to be based on understanding and on "communication." If we all understood each other's *tongue,* then we would be able to get along together. But is it the "gift of tongues" that brings love? Hardly. Even if one had the ability to speak like angels and had no love, he would sound only like the noise of the clanging cymbal, a sound so familiar in pagan temples. The only basis for good human relations, whether public relations, international relations, marital relations, church relations, racial relations, or interpersonal relations, is love—Christian love.

This is particularly pertinent today at a time when men are everywhere sowing the seeds of hate. So many books coming off the press in recent years which deal with national and international problems and race relations are books of hate. Unfortunately, too, many of those who in our day are being lauded for their attempts to bring about changes in society are prophets of hate. I Corinthians 13 is not the Revolutionary's Manifesto. There can be no *lasting* good resulting from words and deeds of hatred which stir men to violence, however good their motives are said to be. There is only one way that really works, and that is the way of love. So even when given the pragmatic test, the answer is still Christian love.

We may ruin the cadence of this beautiful love lyric by attempting to catalog the various manifestations of Christian love, but it is still good to see what the list looks like. The items mentioned could well become a personal inventory, a kind of check list, to see what our

"L.Q." or "Love Quotient" is. Here then is the list. How do we measure up?

Christian Love (4-7)

— is kind, gracious, benign
— is very slow to lose patience (Greek: "has a long mind")
— looks for a way to be constructive
— never boils with jealousy
— is not eager to impress
— is not on parade, does not boast
— is not envious
— is not arrogant or conceited
— is never rude or unmannerly
— is not indecent
— is never selfish and does not pursue selfish aims
— does not insist on its rights
— bears no malice
— is not quickly provoked
— does not keep a record of others' wrongs
— does not take offense easily
— is not irritable or resentful
— is not touchy
— does not feel good when others go wrong
— is always glad when truth comes out on top
— overlooks faults in others
— has unquenchable faith in others
— is always slow to expose, always eager to believe the best
— can face anything—has no limit to its endurance
— is always hopeful
— will never come to an end

The well-known commentator Clarke wrote: "The love of God and of our neighbor for God's sake, is patient towards all men. It suffers all the weakness, ignorance, errors, and infirmities of the children of God, and all the malice and wickedness of the children of this world, and all this, not merely for a time, but long, without end . . ."

Love and Prophecy, Love and Tongues, Love and Knowledge (8-12)

Christian love will be needed *always*—it will never pass away. It is a grace that has currency in two worlds. It is of the very essence of heaven and God.

Prophecy and tongues have an earthly and temporal character. Prophecy, which is an attempt to unfold **8-10** God's plan to man, and tongues, whether actual languages or ecstatic utterances, will no longer be needed in the presence of God. Knowledge, the quest of man, will be set aside for FULL KNOWLEDGE. As it is now human knowledge is but fragmentary, and prophecy too is incomplete because of our limited comprehension of God.

The fuller revelation reminds one of the process of **11, 12** maturity. As a child we did the best we could with our limitations, we *reasoned* and *talked like children.* (Once again the gifts of *knowledge* and *tongues* are hinted at.) But in manhood these earlier modes of thought and communication were replaced with wisdom and seasoned articulation of that wisdom. Our present insights and knowledge are like looking into a smudged or imperfect mirror. (Corinth was noted for its highly polished metal looking glasses, which at the best, however, revealed indistinct images.) Some day, though, we shall no longer see the distorted reflections of the *real.* Then we shall see reality face to face.

The Christian life moves toward fulfillment, which is one of the most exciting things about being a Christian. The Christian view of history is dynamic—always moving toward a goal. At present we understand but little of God or of the many mysteries of earth. But then *everything* will be unfolded. And seeing Christ face to face will be the crowning experience of all time!

As we recognize God and He recognizes us, we shall understand Him as clearly as He understands us! Phillips' translation gives this interpretation: "At present all I know is a little fraction of the truth, but the time will come when I shall know it as fully as God now knows me!"

Three Cardinal Graces That Have Abiding Relevance (13)

13 As a grand conclusion to this great hymn of love we are reminded of the "three graces" that have abiding relevance in terms of peace and happiness here and hereafter. But love outshines both FAITH AND HOPE, which have a temporal character. LOVE will endure forever.

FOR GOD IS LOVE!

CHAPTER XIV

FRUITFUL COMMUNICATION

Before continuing this study one should refer again to the context of the preceding chapters, and particularly to the chart at the beginning of chapter 12.

Place and Purpose of the Gift of Tongues (1-25)

1, 5 "Rather that ye may prophesy" is the key to the interpretation of chapter 14. This very clearly places "tongues," the most-sought-after gift in the Corinthian Church, in its proper position in the gifts scale. Chapter 12, which lists the various *gifts, operations,* and *services,* of the Spirit, places "tongues" and "interpretation of tongues" at the end of the two lists, and concludes: "But covet earnestly the best gifts; and yet shew I unto you a more excellent way." The more excellent way is the way of Christian love, portrayed in the beautiful love lyric of chapter 13 where Paul shows love as superior to any gift.

(Eph. 4: 8-13) Tongues is not mentioned in the list of gifts in Paul's letter to the Ephesians.

Chapter 14 sets forth "prophecy" as the most-to-be-

116

desired gift, comparing it at great length with speaking in tongues. "Greater is he that prophesieth than he that 5 speaketh in tongues, except he interpret that the church may receive edifying." In "tongues," says Paul, there is no edifying. The comparison between "prophecy" and "tongues" is significant from the fact that they duplicate each other, whereas there is no duplication among the other "gifts," "operations," and "services." Since they do duplicate each other, Paul is showing how "prophecy," as a means of communicating the message of God, is a far more efficient and more fruitful way of edifying the church. The ratio of 5 words to 10,000 words indicates the difference in their respective effectiveness as a means of communication.

Why the Gift of Prophecy Is Better Than the Gift of Tongues

Note that the gift of tongues includes *speaking, singing,* and *praying* in tongues, an idea generally disregarded in modern "glossalalia" movements (14:13-15).

1. He that speaks in a tongue (ecstatic) speaks not to 2 men but to God. It then becomes merely an act of personal devotion which might more appropriately be done in the privacy of one's secret chambers.
2. He that prophesies speaks to men in a way that 3 helps to build the church of Christ:

Paul defines "prophecy" as: speaking unto men unto
  - edification (building, instructing)
  - exhortation (warning, advising, encouraging)
  - comfort (giving strength and hope and consolation)

The need in our day for this kind of prophesying is

apparent. The high calling of the Christian counselor is involved in this ministry. Both men and women may prophesy. It can be done—and needs be done—in all those situations where men and women move, and most certainly not only in the sanctuary.

4, 6 3. He that speaks in an unintelligible language edifies himself only, but he that prophesies benefits and builds the church (re-emphasizing the above idea).

4. Prophecy gives no uncertain sound, as does speaking in an unintelligible tongue. It makes sense. It signifies something.

In a day of confusion we need voices that speak in no uncertain sound to call the saints to action in the battle before us. This is not the day for men and women to remain in cloisters to enjoy ecstatic experiences which benefit (?) only the gathered group (and only a small portion of those).

The voices need to be heard in the market place.

9 5. "Prophecy" is easy to understand. Communicating the message to others is an art that needs to be cultivated. Part of our 20th century problem is lack of communication. Music and prayers and sermons that cannot be understood are of no value. Much of our modern ritualistic and polished worship unfortunately does not really communicate to men's spiritual needs.

9 6. Speaking in ecstatic tongues, unless interpreted, is simply to "speak into the air."

11 7. Speaking in tongues is like the speech of the foreigner or the barbarian—it fails to communicate.

14-20 8. "Prophecy" does not divorce the mind or reason from the worship experience. The repeated use of the word "understanding" is significant. While the Christian life is not primarily an intellectual experience, it is also not non-intellectual or irrational.

These verses underscore the true character of Christian worship. It involves "mind" and "spirit." This does not diminish but rather enhances spiritual fervor, for how can anyone get enthusiastic at mere babel. All worship to be fruitful must unite the emotional, esthetic, intellectual, and the spiritual elements in speaking, praying, and singing.

9. Praying or singing in an unintelligible tongue is an unfruitful exercise. Because it cannot be understood it therefore does not increase the ability of the guests in the meeting to follow along intelligently and to join in thanksgiving. **14-17**

10. Five words understood are better than 10,000 not understood. In short, prophesying is 2,000 times better than "tongues." Paul thanked God that he spoke in tongues more than they all, which may have included reference either to his being able to speak in several known languages or in an ecstatic tongue to himself, or to both. He was proficient in Hebrew, Greek, Latin, and Aramaic. But with all his linguistic ability he says he would rather speak five words that are understood than to try to impress people with his many languages. **18, 19**

11. Speaking in tongues immediately shows a lack of maturity. "Be not children in understanding," Paul says. Yet when it comes to "malice," then you should be forgiving like children. **20**

12. "Tongues" were for a special sign to those of the professed chosen people of God who in reality were unbelievers. There is no conflict in these verses, although a first reading seems to suggest that "tongues" were for unbelievers and later that "prophecy" is for unbelievers. The unbelievers for whom it was a sign were Jewish people who refused to believe and to whom God was speaking in a **22-24** **(Isa. 28:11)**

(See later comments in appendix.)

119

strange tongue as Isaiah had predicted.

23
(40)
13. Speaking in tongues sounds like babel and tends toward confusion, while "prophecy" tends toward order and understanding. Clarke reminds us that a lot of modern preaching and singing is unintelligible and is thus actually a form of speaking in strange tongues.

24, 25
14. Prophesying has an evangelistic appeal. Every church service should have a warm drawing appeal. It should never be a cold formal ritualistic or liturgical exercise.

27, 31
15. Prophesying has a wider use. The *whole church* may use the gift of prophecy, whereas speaking in tongues is limited to only three in any given service.

28
16. Prophesying has a further advantage in that no interpreter is required. Interpretation always has its hazards and much of the meaning is lost. Interpretation of tongues can also easily be counterfeited.

32
17. A prophet is always in control of the situation. "The spirits of the prophets are subject to the prophets." There is no such matter as falling down on the floor in a trance, overwhelmed emotionally. A prophet always knows what is going on, knows what he is saying. "A prophet is not merely the mouthpiece but the messenger of God"

Rules to Govern Prophesying or Speaking in Tongues (26-35)

Paul very carefully lays down rules to govern prophecy and speaking in tongues in the public assembly. They are as follows:

12
1. "Seek that ye may excel to the edifying of the church."

13
2. "If you speak in a strange tongue, pray that you may be able to interpret."

3. One must interpret, and if there is no interpreter present, then keep silent. **28**

4. All things should be done with church-building in mind. **26**

5. No more than two or three shall speak in tongues in any given service. **27**

6. All who speak, whether in tongues or in prophecy, must speak in turn. In the case of prophesying, in the Corinthian setting, it seemed to go in courses with two or three speaking and someone following with critical comments. Then others would speak again. Since prophesying is intelligible, it is open to public scrutiny and those with the gift of discernment are able to judge whether the things that are spoken are sound. **27-31**

7. All were permitted to prophesy in a given service. The indication is that there was a need for many, with their varied insights, to contribute in some way to the meeting, so that all present might "learn" (something) and that all might be "comforted." Everyone has special needs, and sometimes these needs can be met best by others in the meeting besides the leader or pastor. This it seems is a missing element in too many services today. There is a kind of "group therapy" derived from attending a church where men's personal needs are high on the agenda. **31**

    (26)

8. The women are to keep silent. This has been interpreted variously. Some apply this only to tongues since we do read elsewhere of Philip's daughters who prophesied and of other women who exercised this gift. Others limit this to the local situation at Corinth, but this is hardly the proper interpretation in view of Paul's similar admonition to Timothy. That passage seems to suggest the **34**

    (I Tim. 2:12)

meaning here. Paul wrote to Timothy: "But I suffer not a woman to teach nor to usurp authority over the man." Women were not to occupy the place of the official prophets designated to take charge of the church. In the lists of qualifications for elders and deacons it should be noted that women are not mentioned. The history of the church has supported this interpretation. The modern trend away from this as an outgrowth of the "equal rights movement" for women has dubious foundations.

Two General rules:

39 9. "Covet to prophesy, and forbid not to speak with tongues."

40 10. "Let all things be done decently and in order."

Concluding Comments (36-40)

36 Concluding this discussion Paul forcibly reminds them once more of their arrogant attitudes which needed to come under careful scrutiny. Surely they were not the ones who had originated the Word of God, nor were they its only recipients. This sharp rebuke helps us to believe that what he had written concerning the gifts of prophecy and tongues reflects on their misunderstanding of the exercise of gifts.

37 He tells them that if any man thinks himself to be a "prophet" or "spiritual," he must acknowledge that what he is writing represents the "commandments of the Lord." True prophets could come to no other conclusion. Spiritually-minded persons would share the logic of Paul's insights. Too frequently "tongues movement" people take an opinionated view on the matter of gifts.

38 Paul bluntly tells all such, This is the way it is—take it or leave it. If any man deliberately chooses to remain ignorant, that is to keep a closed mind on the matter, then let him be ignorant!

The moderating balance is struck in Paul's last two **39, 40** statements where it is clear he does not rule out the exercise of the gift of tongues. He was not forbidding it, only discouraging it, for the many reasons given.

"Wherefore, brethren, covet to prophesy, and forbid not to speak with tongues."
"Let all things be done decently and in order."

The chief goal, stated once more, is to make church-building the main objective and to be orderly and Christian in the public assembly.

(For further comments on this chapter see Appendix.)

CHAPTER XV

THE RESURRECTION OF THE DEAD

"God hath both raised up the Lord, and will also raise **(6:14)** up us by his own power."

The Historical Fact of the Resurrection (3-11)

Among all primitive peoples there has been some form of belief in a life after death. Philosophers have tried to conjecture on the nature of this after-life. The seeming despair and futility of earth's existence seems to call for some satisfying answer. Thankfully the Bible supplies this answer, though in detail it does not speak.

The central theme of the Gospel story is the death and resurrection of Christ. The focal point is the resurrection. There is nothing supernatural about death, but there is about the resurrection. Hence the apostles, as is so clearly recorded in the book of the Acts of the

Apostles, invariably began their preaching with an emphatic declaration that "God hath raised up Jesus our Lord," knowing that faith in this supernatural act was essential in their understanding that Jesus was truly the predicted Messiah.

Peter, in his powerful sermon on the Day of Pentecost, said, "Whom God hath raised up, having loosed the pains of death: because it was not possible that he should be holden of it." During the days following the Pentecost event Luke tells us that "with great power gave the apostles witness of the resurrection of the Lord Jesus." They preached first about the manifestation of God's power in the unbelievable event of the resurrection, and then about this same Jesus having been "slain" for their sins. A dead Jesus could never redeem fallen humanity. Faith in the living resurrected Christ was absolutely prerequisite to the acceptance of His atonement through His death. This was exactly the theme of Paul's great salvation text in his letter to the Romans: "That if thou shalt confess with thy mouth the Lord Jesus, and shalt believe in thine heart that God hath raised him from the dead, thou shalt be saved."

(Acts 2:24)

(Acts 4:33)

(Rom. 10:9)

Chapter 15 of Paul's letter to the Corinthians remains the classic passage on the Christian's grand theme of hope which has been the answer to man's existential despair through the centuries.

Paul tells us that the divine proclamation through preaching is the chief technique by which all men will be saved. Keeping in memory—or holding fast—the Gospel suggests a certain substance or *content* to the Gospel which has saving power. It is not a mystical "resurrection experience" that is the keystone of the Christian faith, but belief in the historical event. Personal faith in this supernatural event is crucial. Regarding the resurrection story as merely a part of legendary "salvation

1-4

history" and relinquishing one's simple faith in the real event can be disastrous. In Paul's day already certain ones had erred concerning resurrection doctrine saying that the resurrection of saints had already taken place. Through this they overthrew the faith of some.

(II Tim. 2:18)

Paul, as Peter, makes it clear that all this was "according to the Scriptures," meaning, "according to the predictions of the prophets and according to God's plan." Peter had said at Caesarea, "To him give all the prophets witness that through his name whosoever believeth in him shall receive remission of sins."

3, 4

(Acts 10:43)

Jesus' actual bodily resurrection is attested by the fact that He was seen after His entombment by a number of individuals and groups: Cephas, James, the "twelve" (actually the eleven, the number 12 being used to signify the total group of Christ's specially chosen number), and the 500 brethren at one time, many of whom were still alive at the time of his writing, 55 A.D.

5, 6, 7

Paul, as "one born out of due time," had seen Christ too on the road to Damascus at the time of his conversion. Though himself an apostle—number 13—he always regarded himself as unworthy of this post because of his previous hatred of Christians and his persecution against them. But the grace of God had made him what he was, and he had nothing of which to boast. In any case, whether it was the original twelve or Paul himself, the Gospel they preached was the same, and it was through them that the Corinthians came to believe. Paul uses four expressions to describe their experience: they had received it; they stood upon it (that is, their faith rested in it); they believed it; they were saved by it.

8

9

10

11

1, 2, 11

Paul spends considerable time laying the groundwork for the message which is to follow. Some of the Corinthians doubted the resurrection; yet how could they when this had been the foundation of their faith in Christ? As already indicated, their doubting was not to be the last in the history of the Christian church.

The resurrection as a fact of history has been challenged in our time—sadly, in many cases, by men who have been acclaimed theologians. Modern religious liberalism either rejects, or at least questions, the actual bodily resurrection of Jesus Christ, the fact which Paul so solidly affirms. Rudolph Bultmann, for example, rejects the passages which are used in the New Testament as "supposed proof" of the miraculous event. For him these were "later embellishments" of the primitive "tradition." He insists that Paul knew nothing of these. Paul's listing of eye-witnesses in I Corinthians 15 he calls a "dangerous procedure," which he says Karl Barth has also shown. Barth seeks to explain away the real meaning of this noted chapter by contending that the list of eye-witnesses was put in, not to prove the fact of the resurrection, but to prove that the preaching of the apostle was like the preaching of the first Christians, the preaching of Jesus as risen Lord! Bultmann insists that "an historical fact which involves a resurrection from the dead is utterly inconceivable" (Bultmann: *Kerygma and Myth,* New York: Harper and Bros., 1961, 38, 39). Statements of this sort can be multiplied over and over. We are living in an age when the very men who should be preaching the Gospel of faith (posited in the resurrection) are preaching the doctrine of doubt.

Very clearly Peter in his message at Caesarea in the house of Cornelius proclaimed:

(Acts 10:38-42)   "How God anointed Jesus of Nazareth with the Holy Ghost and with power: who went about doing good, and healing all that were oppressed of the devil; for God was with him.

"And we are witnesses of all things which he did both in the land of the Jews and in Jerusalem; whom they slew and hanged on a tree;

"Him God raised up the third day, and showed him openly; not to all the people, but unto witnesses chosen before of God, even to us, who did eat and drink with him after he rose from the dead.

"And he commanded us to preach unto the people, and to testify that it is he which was ordained of God to be the Judge of quick (living) and dead."

Paul's Masterful Defense of the Gospel of the Resurrection (1, 2, 12-19)

In the style of a professional lawyer Paul presents his case, point by point. He argues: You have **1, 2** rested your faith on the resurrection, and your very affirmation indicates that either you were deceived in the first place or that you pretended a faith you didn't possess ("believed in vain"). Or was it true that they had had a real faith in the resurrection but were now ready to repudiate it? Putting it another way, You believed in the resurrection once—were you wrong then or now? He continues:

1. If Christ be preached that He rose from the dead **12** (from death), how can you now say there is no resurrection of the dead?

2. Or, to reverse it, If there is no resurrection, then **13** we know that Christ never rose.

3. But if Christ did not rise, then he had been wrong **14** preaching this kind of message in the first place and the faith they had was worthless.

Note the triangle formed by the *fact* of the resurrection, the *preaching* of this fact, and the *believing* in this fact.

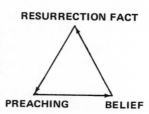

RESURRECTION FACT

PREACHING   BELIEF

127

15   Furthermore, if the resurrection did not take place, then those who testified have been false witnesses.

To repeat:

17   4. If the dead rise not, then Christ is not raised.

18   5. If Christ did not rise, then their faith was vain and they were yet in their sins. And sadly, all who had died "are perished" because they had also believed in vain. To die without hope is to live without hope, which is to be "of all men most miserable." Despair issues from hopelessness.

20   The Christian affirmation is solidly: "BUT NOW IS CHRIST RISEN FROM THE DEAD, AND BECOME THE FIRSTFRUITS OF THEM THAT SLEPT."

The Doctrine of the Resurrection (20-23)

Paul now develops more fully the doctrine of the resurrection. As already noted, the *doctrine* of the resurrection grows out of the *fact* of the resurrection. There is no such matter as basing a doctrine on myth, whatever cryptic language may be used to lend sophistication to such teaching. Neither is there room for any artificial distinctions as Barth attempted to make between *Historie* (the actual event), and *Heilsgeschichte* a mythological realm of so-called "salvation history," a Christian conception of purported events. Certainly nothing can be more real than the real!

Stated briefly the doctrine of the resurrection runs like this:

1. Our salvation is based on a personal belief in the fact of the death and resurrection of Christ.
2. The resurrection theme is central to the *Kerygma* (Gospel proclamation).
3. The resurrection of Christ and of the saints is interdependent—the first makes the second possible; the second affirms the truth of the first.

128

4. The resurrection is the basis of Christian hope.

Paul in his letter to the Romans explains more fully the meaning of faith in the resurrection as the basis of justification or of having God's approval. He says that as Abraham's faith was "imputed" (credited) to him for righteousness, so our faith in "Him that raised up Jesus our Lord from the dead" will be credited to us for righteousness. This then becomes the basis of our justification before God. He continues, "Therefore being justified by faith, we have peace with God through our Lord Jesus Christ . . ." (Rom. 4:24, 25; 5:1)

In all of this the centrality of the resurrection theme is inescapable, and in every case it is based on the creditability of the historical event. Just as science professes to base its "propositions" on empirical data, so Christianity bases its doctrines on empirical data. There is no line of irrationality separating science from faith, as modern philosophy and theology have drawn to make their theories palatable to the modern mind. There is no "leap of faith" needed where the scrutable facts of history compel one to believe.

But the doctrine is not based *only* on the historical event but on simple logic. Since death came by one man (Adam), then life must again come by man to vindicate the "life principle" above the "death principle." In Freud's outlook on life, the death principle would be victorious. Paul writes: "For since by man came death, by man came also the resurrection of the dead." "For as in Adam all die, even so in Christ shall all be made alive." 21 22

Here we deal with some hard facts: Adam, the first man, sinned, and through this death passed to all men. Man is a reality. Death is a reality. AND IF THE BIBLE IS TRUE, and we believe that it is, *the resurrection is also a reality.*

This defines the doctrine of the resurrection a little further: The resurrection is the eschatological fulfillment of all that was lost in Eden.

23   The order of the resurrection is now described: Christ was the firstfruits of the resurrection. The saints will be raised at His coming.

The term "firstfruits" has its origin in the Old (Lev. 23: Testament feast of the harvest when the priest offered 9-21) the wave-sheaf offering as a token of the early harvest. The passover which immediately preceded this represented Calvary. This was followed by the regular Sabbath, and then "on the morrow after the Sabbath," the priest waved a sheaf of grain before the Lord. The three days from Calvary to Easter morning are thus set forth in type. The very fact that it was *on the morrow after the Sabbath,* denotes Jesus as the firstfruits of the spiritual harvest, being raised on the first day of the (16:1) week, the foundation of the observance of the "Lord's Day" in the Christian church. Counting forward from that day the Law reads, "Seven sabbaths shall be complete: even unto the morrow after the sabbath shall ye number fifty days." On this (fiftieth) day the late harvest was again to be celebrated with a wave-sheaf offering. This corresponds to the Day of Pentecost in the New Testament, which took place exactly fifty days after the Resurrection. Christ was thus the firstfruits of the great spiritual harvest which took place on the Day of Pentecost—the "later harvest." But in another sense, of course, He was also the first fruits of the resurrection to which the book of Revelation refers. It (Rev. 14:15) speaks there of the angels thrusting in their sickles to (See also reap—"for the time is come . . . to reap; for the harvest James 5:7) of the earth is ripe."

Eschatology (The doctrine of last things) (24-28)

We have already stated that the doctrine of the Resurrection is part of the eschatology of the New Testament. He carries this process of final fulfillment further: "Then cometh the end, when he shall have delivered up the kingdom to God, even the Father; when **24** he shall have put down all rule and all authority and power." Opinions differ as to the nature of Christ's kingdom, some believing that the word "kingdom" is merely a designation for Christ's present rule in the hearts of men. Others say it represents the church itself. But the language here indicates more than a description of the church or of the Christian life. There is a time factor very evident in the above statement of Paul. At a given point in history Christ will deliver to God an entity—the kingdom. That His kingdom has political dimensions is shown in the last part of the above quotation. He must first put down all (earthly) rule and power and authority. Some interpret this to mean the putting down of the principalities and powers of Satan's spiritual kingdom. It is these same demonic powers, of **(Eph. 1:21, 22)** course, which also operate in and control the earthly kingdoms, so that whatever the interpretation, this act of the resurrection and final end of all earthly and satanic power marks the end of one age and the beginning of another. This is exactly what Paul is trying to declare—that man's existence does not end at the grave. "In the dispensation of the fulness of times he [will] gather together in one all things in Christ, both **(Eph. 1:10)** which are in heaven, and which are on earth . . . " and "in the ages to come [God will] show the exceeding riches of his grace in his kindness toward us through **(Eph. 2:7)** Christ Jesus."

The book of Revelation speaks of "the kingdoms of this world *becoming* the kingdoms of our Lord and of **(Rev. 11:15)** his Christ," and whatever the interpretation in terms of prophetic fulfillment, it is clear that it is set within the framework of the time factor. Somewhere on the chronological scale, at a given point in history, Christ **26-28** will intervene and all things will be put under His feet **25** and be "subdued." The last enemy to be destroyed will be death. The resurrection of Christ itself was a victory over death, but did not end death in mankind. The fruits of the resurrection will not be fully realized until the end of time when Christ becomes King of Kings and Lord of Lords over earthly and heavenly powers.

Baptized for the Dead (29)

29   One commentator has called verse 29, which speaks of being "baptized for the dead," the most difficult verse in the New Testament. This writer does not concur, although admittedly it poses an interesting problem of interpretation. It reads, "Else what shall they do which are baptized for the dead, if the dead rise not at all? why are they then baptized for the dead?"

Whatever difficulty encountered here arises from the language, not the real intent of Paul's teaching.

Paul is simply saying, why worry about the dead if nothing further awaits them? Some churches have used this passage as a basis for actual baptism for dead persons who have died outside of Christ. The entire teaching of the New Testament in no way supports such a doctrine since the whole plan of redemption and personal acceptance of Christ would be set aside. Evangelism would lose its meaning since it would be very simple to have Christians now living to be baptized for all the wicked dead, that is, those who were known to be wicked. Yet who knows who that includes, so that in reality, to be on the safe side, one would need to be baptized for just about everyone who is dead except the most widely recognized saints who we are certain died "in the Lord." There is no record that the Early Church ever engaged in the practice of having members baptized for those who had died as unbelievers.

There are several plausible meanings for verse 29. One is, that since Paul mentions the jeopardy they were constantly facing—that is, the danger of persecution and death which all Christians at this time faced in a real way—that they were in essence being baptized *for death.* Jesus had spoken of the baptism of suffering with which His followers needed to be baptized if they were to be one with Him. Why are you willing, Paul says, to be baptized with the baptism of suffering and death if there is no future? Or, "baptized for the dead" could mean that Paul was referring to their desire to be baptized into the body of Christ *for the sake of the dead,* their loved ones, whom they expected some day to meet again. Or, there is still another explanation. Maybe there were some at Corinth who *erroneously* were thinking they could allow themselves to be baptized for their pagan loved ones who had died without a knowledge of Christ. In any case—whatever the interpretation—*the point comes through clearly, Why bother at all about death or the dead if there is no life beyond the grave?*

Why Suffer All the Hardships If There Is No Resurrection? (30-34)

Paul asks the Corinthians, Why go through all the **30** dangers of being a Christian, risking your own lives, if there is no after-life? If they were taking this courageous step as witnesses for Christ (the Greek word for witness is *martus,* from which our word martyr comes, indicating that for many early Christians it meant death to declare themselves for Christ), then how can they say, as some did at Corinth, there is no resurrection?

31 The answer to their living in danger daily is found in the Christian's constant rejoicing in light of a bright future. ("Your rejoicing" in some of the old manuscripts is "our rejoicing.")

32 Did Paul fight real "beasts" at Ephesus as he says? Comparing notes with many sources and trying to (Acts 14: evaluate these, the probability is that he did. We know 6-21) he was once stoned to death or to the point of death, though the first seems more likely if one connects this (II Cor. event with his comments in his second letter to Corinth. 12:1-4) So there may have been other similar events which (II Cor. 1:8) brought him so near death that he despaired even of life.

In any case, again, why go through any of this "if the dead rise not?" If there is no hereafter, why not adopt the Epicurean ideal of "living it up"? The motto of all pleasure seekers is, "Eat and drink; for tomorrow we die."

33 But one must not be lulled to sleep by such false comfort. Associating with those who live in pleasure can soon corrupt one's thinking and outlook on life in its **34** relation to the hereafter. At any rate this is no excuse to sin.

But How Will the Resurrection Take Place? (35-57)

Paul is arguing in a kind of soliloquy, trying to meet **35** the arguments which had apparently been raised by the skeptical Corinthians who doubted the resurrection. First, they had said, There is no resurrection. Now they are asking, Yes, but how could this take place?

Paul uses some earthly miracles accepted as ordinary fact to prove this unusual miracle of the resurrection.

The Greeks believed in a spiritual kind of resurrection in which the spirit, separated from the body, finds its home with God. Paul does not discuss here the immortality of the soul, but takes it for granted. What he is establishing is the resurrection of the body.

The paradox of mid-twentieth century theology is that while it purports to be interested in the needs of the "whole man," it rejects the resurrection of the "whole man," a fact which simply underscores the humanism of their philosophy.

The duality of human nature is not a Platonic idea adopted by Paul or by the Church fathers; it is a distinctly Judeo-Christian concept. "There is a natural **44** body, and there is a spiritual body." To the Thessalonians Paul defines this further by describing man in fact as tripartite—having body, soul, and spirit. Man **(I Thess.** therefore is more than *mere* animal. **5:23)**

Paul uses the earthly miracle of grain dying so that a new life may emerge. It is a very unique description of the resurrection. No one's old bones will inhabit heaven, **36-38** but as sure as God can make a green stalk of wheat out of a dead and disintegrated kernel, so God can make a new *person* out of dead bones.

"But God giveth it a body as it hath pleased him, and to every seed his own body."

In spite of the fact that Christianity deals with things of the Spirit, Christians have always held a high view of the human body. This is evidenced in the care given to those who are in need through sickness or distress. Jesus was much concerned with healing those who were ill and was concerned for the poor, and urged this upon His followers. James and John, as well as Paul himself, stress supplying bodily needs to those who have needs. In the last chapter of this letter he gives instructions on receiving offerings for the poor at Jerusalem.

Likewise, Christians have always held a high view of the sacredness of the body even after death. Smith states that "the early Christians abhorred the pagan fashion of burning their dead in funeral pyres and preserving the ashes in urns. The body was sacred in their eyes, and they committed it reverently to the earth. Reverence was their sole motive, but the pagans imputed to them a fond solicitude to preserve the body intact until it should be reanimated at the resurrection; and it is told that during the persecution in the reign of the Emperor Verus they outraged the bodies of the martyrs at Lyons and Vienne, and then burned them and cast the ashes into the river Rhone that they might have no hope of resurrection. 'Now let us see,' they jeered, 'if they will rise again, and if their God can succor them and snatch them out of our hands' " (Eus History Eccl, V.1, quoted in David Smith: *Life and Letters of St. Paul,* Harper and Bros., N.Y., p. 316).

A second illustration has to do with *kinds* of flesh and kinds of celestial bodies. Paraphrasing Christ's own words, "Thou canst not make one hair white or black," one might say here, "Thou canst not make beasts out of birds or birds out of fishes or change stars into planets." And just so "is the resurrection of the dead." Changes are involved which are inexplicable, though there may be natural counterparts which are observable. As the glory of the terrestrial bodies differs from the celestial, so the glory of the resurrected body differs from the earthly. The earthly body goes down in weakness (or defeat), but is raised in power (victory).

46
47   Adam is the prototype of the natural earthly man—Christ, the Lord from Heaven, is the prototype of the spiritual man.

(I Cor. 2:
14, 15)   This part of the letter turns our mind back again to I Corinthians 2 where Paul discusses the natural man and the spiritual man. "As is the earthy, such are they also that are earthy; and as is the heavenly, such are they also that are heavenly."—Yet all of us who strive to be

spiritual rather than earthy still have the imprint of the   **49**
earthy. One day we shall bear the image of the heavenly.

Flesh and blood cannot inherit the kingdom of God.
Corruption itself cannot be transposed into incorrup-   **50**
tion—hence the need for the resurrection meta-
morphosis. Resurrection is not resuscitation.

Paul in his letter to the church at Philippi speaks of
"knowing Christ" and "the power of his resurrection,"   **(Phil. 3:**
which at least is a foretaste of the physical resurrection.   **10, 11)**
For unless one experiences on earth a changing of life
from the earthy to the spiritual, he will never be able to
"attain unto the resurrection from the dead."

No one will ever enter heaven without first having the   **50**
experience of being spiritually risen with Christ.

In a day when a new humanism is being offered as the
contemporary Gospel—the idea of being "more human"
and having a new reverence for life (Schweitzer) or of
living close to nature—we must remember that the earthy
man in his earthiness is not an eligible candidate for
admission into the kingdom of God.

All men will be raised from the dead, and the nature   **51**
of the resurrection of the wicked dead compared with
that of the righteous dead is not described here. The
wicked dead who are raised will not experience eternal
life, but eternal death—a continuing *existence* of separation from God in endless death.

Paul is speaking here of the resurrection "from among
the dead" and the nature of their resurrection. Not all   **(Phil. 3:11)**
will "sleep" (die) before Jesus comes, but all will be
changed (metamorphosed).

It will be sudden, in an "Augenblick" (German) "the   **52**
twinkling of an eye." The dead will be raised at the
sound of the great trumpet.

For the corruptible saints must put on incorruption   **53**
to be eligible for that kingdom. Mortality and all that

goes with it—disease, sorrow, death, will be exchanged for immortality, permanent health, joy and eternal life.

54
(v. 26)
Death, the last enemy to be destroyed, will be swallowed up in the victory of the resurrection. When Napoleon's armies were seemingly overrunning Europe, there was great fear everywhere of the consequences. On the day of the battle of Waterloo, when Napoleon was pitted against the English general, the Duke of Wellington, across the English Channel on the Chalk Cliffs of Dover men were anxiously watching for smoke signals to announce either defeat or victory. Finally the words came through in code: "Wellington defeated—" The despairing news flashed quickly across England. But a cloud had hidden the complete message. As the cloud lifted, the full message came through—"Wellington defeated Napoleon!" So death, presently seeming so victorious as it brings to an end many careers and removing our loved ones, suddenly itself is "swallowed up" in the victory of the Resurrection.

55
The only ones to experience the sting of death and the sad victory of death are those who have lived in sin.

Final Admonition (58)

58
The "therefores" of the Apostle Paul are impressive. "Therefore, my beloved brethren (his audience who were experiencing the victory of Christ), be ye steadfast, unmoveable, always abounding in the work of the Lord, forasmuch as ye know that your labor is not in vain in the Lord." The sorrows and disappointments of life may be overwhelming, but "it pays to serve Jesus each step of the way." At the end of the road it will have been worth it all.

CHAPTER XVI

SYSTEMATIC GIVING   PERSONAL OBSERVATIONS
PORTRAIT GALLERY   FINAL ADVICE

Systematic Giving (1-4)

Paul closes his letter with some administrative detail, final advice, and personal observations. At the very end are the usual felicitations and the final benediction.

As a church administrator he gives some instructions **1** on the matter of offerings, "orders" which he had also given to all the churches of Galatia. There are some matters which church leaders and pastors need to handle as routine executive detail and others which should be left for congregational decision. The mark of a good administrator is to know when each of these methods is most appropriate and how to use the executive function and "democracy" in the proper balance. This balance is beautifully illustrated in chapter 5 where he deals with church discipline.

The collection for the saints refers to the offering the churches of Achaia (Greece) were to give to the needy saints in Jerusalem. The word "collection" is not a cheap word for a church offering. It is in fact a very precise word to describe the *gathering of personal offerings* at the weekly church service. In this particular case it represented the collection of weekly offerings that Paul would receive when he came on his next visit, the collection he and others would be taking to Jerusalem. Paul did not want any kind of solicitation program or a drumming up of the "giving spirit" after he arrived. Giving should be thought-through and systematic. As we learn here and elsewhere in the New Testament, it was an early Christian practice for churches to help each other and to aid those in need.

"As God hath prospered him," establishes the New

2   Testament system for giving. The basis of giving is to be not only *"proportionate,"* as was the Old Testament tithe (tenth), but *"progressive,"* based on a sliding percentage which is determined by the increase or decrease in one's weekly earnings. Obviously those of high income can afford *more* than the Old Testament legal standard, while those of a very low income may not even be able to afford the tithe.

That the saints from the beginning of the founding of the Christian church observed the "Lord's Day" (the day of the Lord's resurrection) is evidenced by Paul's reference to the "first day of the week." It is therefore not a heathen day of celebration adopted by the Medieval church, or a mistake of the calendar which causes the Christian church today to observe almost universally the first day of the week as the Christian "Sabbath." The names of the days of the week and of the months of the year are unfortunately names of pagan gods in most instances, but the name of the day, as in the case of "Sun" day, does not change the significance of the day. Christians are neither sun nor moon worshippers simply because they call the first and the second days of the week "Sunday" and "Monday" (Moonday), as does society in general which uses the early pagan designations. In reality Christians should call the first day of the week *"Sonday"* or "The Lord's Day."

As noted in the previous chapter, the Old Testament wave sheaf-offerings on the "morrow after the Sabbath" were a prototype of the New Testament Christian Sabbath. It is said that in the Early Church gatherings it was customary for the leader, as part of the opening of the service, to say: "The Lord is risen," to which the congregation would respond in unison: "The Lord is risen indeed!"

That there was need to protect the integrity of the   3
church in money matters is shown in Paul's suggestion to
have several men "approved by letter," to take the
offering to Jerusalem. It might be, he said, that he would
also be able to go with them. It is not that people could   4
not be trusted, but from the very earliest it was
important to safeguard the reputation of the new
"religion" and its method of operating. Probably at no
other point are men in general more critical of church
administration than in financial operations. Paul wanted
no room for suspicion.

Personal Note (5-9)

Paul said he would come to them when he comes   5
back from Macedonia. Maybe he'll spend the winter with
them. He is thinking they might be able to help him on   6
his trip from there. Right now it didn't suit, but he
would like to spend some time with them "if the Lord   7
permit." His whole life was based on God's personal will   (See II Cor.
for him. He made no off-the-cuff decisions. Erdman   1:15-20)
suggests some reasons for his delay. If he came at once,
he might have to deal more severely with the errant
members at Corinth. He wishes to give them time in
which to adjust some of the painful matters to which he
had been referred. The main cause for the delay which
he wishes to stress, however, is the great open door for
service at Ephesus.

He was planning to stay at Ephesus until Pentecost.   8
This interesting reference to Pentecost makes us aware
that the Early Church took special note of the day
which in the centuries to follow was to be celebrated as
"Whitsunday," so named for the white apparel worn on
that day. Interestingly, there is no indication that
Christmas was ever kept as a special day by the Early
Church as we do today. Important as was Christ's birth,

141

probably Pentecost is in a sense more significant than Christmas since it was that day that marked the birthday of the Christian church.

9 Ephesus had proved to be a fruitful place of ministry, but there was also much opposition. We recall the "adversaries" Paul had encountered there.

If Paul had worked only where there was no opposition, he would never have been able to launch his vast missionary program. Often the places of greatest difficulty have been the places of greatest opportunity. For two years he had conducted a kind of off-campus student center in that town where he met with some of the young men from the "university" who reasoned or disputed with him in a kind of formal situation concerning the various philosophies of the day. His ministry here proved to be very effective.

The Portrait Gallery (10-19)

Appended to a number of Paul's Epistles are the lists of individuals he knew personally. He had a remarkable memory for names and also a due regard for each person's contribution to the work. Note the persons he names here:

10 1. Timotheus (Timothy) — Paul's companion and assistant pastor-at-large, he says, "worketh the work of the Lord."

2. Apollos — Paul's co-pastor at Corinth was not downgraded by Paul because of some apparent rivalry. He says, "I greatly desired him to come unto you."

15, 16
(12:5, 28;
Rom. 16:3;
Acts 18:2,
18, 26)

3. The family of Stephanus — They, Paul says, are "addicted" (devoted) to the ministry of the saints—evidently in the area of *diakonia* such as Aquila and Priscilla who also were "helps." Stephanus is included in another list with

142

4. Fortunatus and   **17**
5. Achaicus, all of whom were helpers of one sort or
   another. Paul says "that which was lacking on
   your part they have supplied," and that "they
   have refreshed my spirit and yours." Paul urges
   the church to "acknowledge" these men for   **18**
   their contribution.

Timothy was a fine young "prophet" who was   **10**
thoroughly dedicated to the task for which God had
called him. Paul regarded him as his "spiritual son." Although perhaps a bit of an introvert or over-sensitive and
without the eloquence of Apollos or the boldness of
Paul, Paul noted that "he worketh the work of the
Lord," which was the all-important matter. He did not
want him to come to them too timid to take up his tasks
at Corinth, and he kindly chides the Corinthians who
were so judgmental of leaders, that they were not to
"despise him but conduct him forth in peace." He was
looking for him "with the brethren," evidently the ones
he was expecting to come with the offering.   **11**

He had wanted Apollos to come too, but Apollos he
says was not "minded at all!" to come at this time. Some
have interpreted the Greek text here to mean that it was
not in the will of the Lord that he should come at this   **12**
time, rather than being a matter of strong personal
feeling. At any rate, he would come whenever the door
opened. Paul was not the kind of person to assign wrong
motives to anyone.

Now, as a field commander issuing order to his men,   **13**
Paul addresses himself directly to his beloved parishoners
in a final salute and charge:

"Watch ye, stand fast in the faith, quit (acquit) you   **14**
(yourselves) like men, be strong. Let all things be done
with charity."

What more noble command—and appeal—could any

143

leader make to his people when he knew that his time with them would not be long and that it was they who would have to carry on in his absence? This challenge rings down through the centuries to all Christians for all time. There is nothing weak or namby-pamby about the Christian life and ministry!

It was exactly on this kind of robust, rigorous faith that Paul's missionary program was founded and upon which it grew. His command, backed by his own example, undoubtedly served as a constant motivation to all who may have had any tendency to weaken along the way. Again we note the great need at Corinth—that whatever their service, the underlying basis of operation was to be charity (love).

19 One of the churches of Asia was that of the church in the house of Aquila and Priscilla. There seem to have been some personal connections here with Paul at this point so that he includes them in his final salutation—"Aquila and Priscilla salute you much in the Lord with the church that is in their house." Where they were at this time is not clear, but maybe with Paul. All the
20 other brethren at Philippi from where this letter was written sent greetings at this time.

Final Advice (20-22)

And then he says—"Greet ye one another with an holy kiss." This command is mentioned five times in Paul's writings. It was an early practice of the church, a form of salutation—men with men, women with women, and there are churches to this day which take this as a command to be observed. It is certainly no less meaningful than the kiss of friendship or the kiss of filial and parental love practiced among all peoples. It is one of the most meaningful ways Christians have of expressing *agape* in the brotherhood context.

Though Paul's letters were written by an amenuensis **21** (secretary) he now affixes his own signature and adds some personal remarks.

And what a wonderful way of closing a letter, **22** following his command to express their love to each other, when he says, "If any man love *not* the Lord Jesus Christ, let him be *Anathema Maranatha.*" Anathema means accursed. Earlier he had told them that "no man **(12:3)** speaking by the Spirit of God calleth Jesus accursed," so that what he is saying here essentially is: If you love not Christ, it is evident that you have not the Spirit of God, and therefore *you* are the accursed. *Maranatha* was an early form of Christian greeting or farewell: "The Lord is at hand." They were constantly reminding each other of the imminent possibility of His return, another motivation for careful living.

The Benediction (23-24)

And now the final benediction: "The grace of our **23** Lord Jesus Christ be with you. My love be with you all in Christ Jesus. Amen."

Contrasted with "if any man love not," Paul says, *"My love* is with you." Closing with the name of Christ and His love and grace is a fitting conclusion to this most notable letter to the Church at Corinth. Amen.

APPENDIX

Additional Comments on Speaking in Tongues in the New Testament

There are four other places in the New Testament where speaking in tongues is mentioned. There is some question as to the exact meaning of the word "tongues" as it is used in these passages. There are those who insist that they all refer to the same kind of experience and others who say Acts 2 refers to known languages, while I Corinthians 14, Acts 10 and 19 and Mark 16 refer to strange or ecstatic tongues. The word "unknown" preceding the word tongues in the King James version of I Corinthians 14 does not occur there in the Greek New Testament.

(Acts 2:1-18; 10:46)
(Mk. 16:17, 18)

Mark 16:17, 18

> And these signs shall follow them that believe; In my name shall they cast out devils; they shall speak with new tongues; They shall take up serpents; and if they drink any deadly thing, it shall not hurt them; they shall lay hands on the sick, and they shall recover.

Acts 2:

> On the day of Pentecost "there appeared unto them cloven tongues like as of fire and it sat upon each of them. And they were all filled with the Holy Ghost and began to speak with other tongues, as the Spirit gave them utterance . . .

There were at Jerusalem Jews "out of every nation under heaven" for that occasion, and they were confounded "because that every man heard them speak in his own language." They marvelled and said to each other:

> Behold, are not all these which speak Galileans? And how hear we every man in our own tongue, wherein we were born?

147

They were all amazed, but some were in doubt as to the meaning of all this. Peter then explained this event as the fulfilling of the Old Testament prophet Joel who had prophesied:

(Acts 2: 17, 18)

(Joel 2:28)

> And it shall come to pass in the last days, saith God, I will pour out of my Spirit upon all flesh: and your sons and your daughters shall prophesy, and your young men shall see visions, and your old men shall dream dreams; and on my servants and on my handmaidens I will pour out in those days of my Spirit and they shall prophesy . . .

Acts 10:44-46

> While Peter yet spake these words, the Holy Ghost fell on all them which heard the word. And they of the circumcision (Jews) which believed were astonished, as many as came with Peter, because on the Gentiles also was poured out the gift of the Holy Ghost. For they heard them speak with tongues, and magnify God.

Acts 19:6

> And when Paul had laid his hands upon them, the Holy Ghost came on them: and they spake with tongues and prophesied.

Several things should be noted in the above passages. In the first place, this was not the gift of "ears," as some have suggested, but the gift of tongues. Mark had predicted that a time would come when men would *speak* with new tongues, and Luke tells us in Acts that they began to *speak* with other tongues, the apparent fulfillment of this. Those who heard were amazed that they heard those gathered disciples *speak* in their own languages. It is also clear that on the Day of Pentecost they spoke specific known languages. The scriptures in Acts 10 and Acts 19 do not make it clear whether these were known languages.

Interestingly, the prophecy of Joel which Peter said was being fulfilled before their eyes, referred not to speaking in tongues, but to prophesying. In other words, the people on the Day of Pentecost were *prophesying in* various *tongues!* These were tongues used then in the various parts of the world named in Acts 2. This whole experience compares so completely with the theme of I Corinthians 14 where prophecy is upheld as a better gift because it is intelligible.

The Pentecost event and the "tongues" experiences at Corinth of whatever sort were both the fulfillment of another prophecy. Paul wrote: "In the law it is written, **(14:21)** With men of other tongues and other lips will I speak unto this people; and yet for all that will they not hear me, saith the Lord." Isaiah's prophecy is what is quoted here. Sometimes the prophets were included in the general category of the "law." Isaiah had predicted that **(Isa. 28:11)** because of the hardness of the people's hearts, the time would come when God would speak to his people "with stammering lips and another tongue." This was to be a special sign or warning to those of the Jewish people who failed to respond to God's overtures of grace.

As the Gospel spread, the story of that marvelous Pentecost event also spread, and it is altogether possible that the Corinthians, in trying to emulate that memorable experience—some had no doubt been there—spoke in ecstatic tongues with no man being able to understand them. In itself this was nothing to be condemned so long as it was done "decently and in order."

Paul was not condemning this but recognized it as a bona fide working of the Spirit, which however, communicated to God and not to men unless interpreted.

Opinions vary as to whether the gift of tongues or in fact any of the gifts mentioned in chapter 12, terminated with the close of the New Testament period or whether they were to continue to the end of time. There are those who feel there was a special period—the apostolic age—when some special manifestations were needed for the confirmation of the Gospel, and like the apostleship itself, passed away with that age.

(Acts 10) The repetition of the Pentecost experience in the home of Cornelius at Caesarea, sometimes referred to as the "Gentile Pentecost," gives support to this idea. The people who had come with Peter were astonished, as they heard them speak in tongues, that "on the Gentiles also was poured out the gift of the Holy Ghost." The two occasions, the "Jewish Pentecost," and the "Gentile Pentecost," fulfilled Joel's prophecy and made everyone aware that this was indeed the beginning of a new age when salvation was to be made available to all men. Isaiah's prophecy showed that God was speaking to the Jews in a strange tongue showing that God was speaking through Christ, who was indeed the Messiah. It was a special message for them. The historical event of speaking in tongues was thus an important stage in helping to initiate the New Covenant.

Whatever position one takes on the gift of tongues, it must be noted that Paul closed his letter by saying, "Covet to prophesy, and forbid not to speak in tongues."

So then, if this involves a known language interpreted under a special working of the Spirit, or an ecstatic tongue, so long as God is being glorified it cannot be condemned. Actually there is no pastor who would not be happy to know that his members were living in such close communion with God that they were having ecstatic moments with Him in their secret prayer chambers. Or if they experienced similar moments of ecstacy in the public assembly and behaved in an orderly manner, again he would not feel disturbed. This is probably what Paul meant when he said, "I would that ye all spake with tongues." The deadness of most

150

churches today is an index of a lack of personal experience with Christ on the part of many members, a lack of the full indwelling of the Spirit.

However, it is difficult to understand how it has come about through the years that a passage of Scripture which so definitely stresses the advantage of prophecy over tongues, should ever have been misconstrued to mean the exact opposite. There are some who claim that one must be able to speak in tongues to prove that he has had the "baptism of the Spirit." Such a position is totally unwarranted. Certainly no one would insist that the other signs mentioned by Mark should also be evidenced in every life, namely, the taking up of poisonous snakes or the drinking of poison without harm.

There is an inescapable connection between the "puffed-up" Christians at Corinth who were fleshly and sensual, and their avid zeal for practicing spectacular gifts.

Speaking in tongues is also invariably an experience of the "gathered group" and is group-centered. The various "operations" and "services," part of the Spirit-manifestations of chapter 12, have a practical use that can have far wider relevance in the "scattered group" and in the world at large. For that reason it might be good to think more in terms of "prophecy movements," since there are still so many who have not heard for the first time the Good News. And there are also so many today who need the kind of personal counselling implied in the New Testament word "prophecy"—exhortation, edification and comfort.

There can be a subtle form of self-righteousness and "class distinction" in any situation where certain ones can claim a particular gift which is labelled as a mark of a special "baptism." Furthermore as one respected

151

commentator has pointed out, there is a danger in exercising a gift that can so easily be counterfeited. Ecstatic tongues are not open to the same kind of objective scrutiny suggested in "discerning of spirits" or in searching the Scriptures, as the Bereans did, to find out if the things Paul spoke were true.

Some Comments on Worship Services

There is probably no place in the New Testament where the manner of conducting a service is spelled out as explicitly as in I Corinthians 14. One would think that as Christians fell under the influence of the Holy Spirit there would be complete freedom, and there would be no structuring of the services. Quite the opposite is suggested here. Paul's careful discussion indicates the dangers connected with the use of tongues. He was concerned with safeguarding this gift so that the public would not get wrong impressions of the new "religion." God after all is a God of order.

A word should be said, however, about the typical modern church service which too frequently is a dead affair. Not enough happens today in the public assembly. In the elite churches there is an attempt made to cater to the refined tastes of the more elegant worshippers, who in a typical service file in and occupy their pews while someone sings and prays and preaches. All is carefully timed and carried out. In the less formal churches there is still too much formality, though perhaps more audience participation. The wheels turn with a certain deadly precision as songs are sung, offerings lifted, and sermons preached. There is not much room for spontaneity—for the "psalm," the "revelation" or the word of testimony. Everything is too well planned.

If it is true that the "holiness" churches are taken up

too much with the noisy or ecstatic elements, it is just as true that the general run of churches are too silent, stifled by form and meaningless ritual. As someone has so aptly said, the modern church is not dying with "fever" but with "anemia." The tragedy is that there seems to be little exercise of any of the gifts, operations, and services. The waste of talent in the average church today is appalling. The clear indication in chapter 14 is that if one had a "psalm," a "doctrine," a "tongue," an "interpretation," there was enough liberty that he could freely participate, sharing his spiritual experience with the congregation.

The radical departure today from the formal worship service is an indication of the hunger of many for more opportunity to give vocal expression to their faith. Unfortunately, many modern worship idioms are not a witness to the "life of God in the soul," but merely a "sounding brass and a tinkling cymbal," "trumpets with uncertain sounds," and harps and pipes without discernible tunes.

BIBLIOGRAPHY

Benson, Joseph. *Benson's Commentary, Vol. V, Romans–Revelation.* New York: T. Carlton and J. Porter.

Berry, George Ricker. *The Interlinear Translation of the Greek New Testament,* with Greek–English Lexicon. Hinds and Noble, 1897.

Bultmann, Rudolf Carl. *Kerygma and Myth,* a Theological Debate. New York: Harper and Row Publishers, 1961.

Clarke, Adam. *The New Testament of Our Lord and Saviour Jesus Christ.* New York: Abingdon Press.

Cook, F. C., Ed. *The Bible Commentary.* New York: Scribners, 1886.

Davis, Jack. *Let Her Be Veiled.* New York: Carlton Press, 1967.

Davis, John D.; Gehman, Henry Snyder. *The Westminster Dictionary of the Bible.* Philadelphia: The Westminster Press, 1944.

Dayton, Wilber T., et. al. *Wesleyan Bible Commentary (Vol. V).* Grand Rapids: William B. Eerdmans Publishing Co., Copyright 1965.

Demaray, Donald E. *Handbook of the Bible.* Los Angeles: Cowman Pub. Co., 1964.

Dods, Marcus. *The Expositors Bible.* W. R. Nicoll, Editor, Grand Rapids, Michigan: Wm. B. Eerdmans Publishing Company.

Ellicott, C. J. *Commentary on I Corinthians.* Longmans, Green and Co., 1897.

Erdman, Charles R. *The First Epistle of Paul to the Corinthians.* Philadelphia: The Westminster Press.

Foreman, Kenneth J. *The First Letter of Paul to the Corinthians,* Vol. 21 of *The Layman's Bible Commentary.* Balmer H. Kelley, Ed., Richmond: John Knox Press, 1961.

Godet, F. *Commentary on I Corinthians.* Translated by A. Cusin, T. and T. Clarke, 1887.

Green, James Benjamin. *Studies in the Holy Spirit.* New York: Fleming H. Revell Co., 1936.

Jameison, Robert; Fausset, A. R.; and Brown, David. *A Commentary, Critical and Explanatory* (Vol. II). Hartford: S. S. Scranton Co., 1873.

Latourette, K. S. *A History of Christianity.* New York: Harper and Bros., 1953.

Lehman, Chester K. *The Holy Spirit and the Holy Life.* Scottdale, Pa.: Herald Press, 1959.

Lenski, R. C. H. *The Interpretation of St. Paul's First and Second Epistle to the Corinthians.* Columbus, Ohio: © Wartburg Press, 1946.

Miller, Paul M. *The Prayer Veiling.* Indiana-Michigan Mennonite Conference, 1953.

Morris, Leon. *The First Epistle of Paul to the Corinthians.* Grand Rapids, Mich.: Wm. B. Eerdmans Publishing Co., Copyright, The Tyndale Press, 1963.

Ringenberg, Loyal R. *The Word of God in History.* Butler, Indiana: Higley Press, 1953.

Robertson, A. T. *Paul, the Interpreter of Christ.* Nashville, Tenn.: Broadman Press, 1921.

Robertson, A. T. *Word Pictures in the New Testament,* (Vol. IV, The Epistles of Paul). Nashville, Tenn.: Broadman Press, 1930.

Schaeffer, Francis. *Escape From Reason.* Downers Grove, Illinois: Intervarsity, 1968.

Shepard, J. W. *The Life and Letters of St. Paul.* Grand Rapids, Mich.: Wm. B. Eerdmans Publishing Co., 1950.

Smith, David. *Life and Letters of St. Paul.* New York: Harper and Bros.

Stalker, James. *The Life of St. Paul.* Old Tappan, N.J.: Fleming H. Revell Co.

Stauffer, John L. *The Baptism and Filling of the Holy Spirit.* Harrisonburg, Va.: Sword and Trumpet.

Unger, Merrill F. *The Baptizing Work of the Holy Spirit.* Wheaton, Ill.: Van Kampen Press, 1953.

Vincent, Marvin R. *Word Studies in the New Testament* (Vol. II, The Epistles of Paul). Grand Rapids, Mich.: Wm. B. Eerdmans Publishing Co., 1946.

Weidner, Revere Franklin. *Biblical Theology of the New Testament,* Vol. II. New York: Fleming H. Revell Co., 1891.

Wenger, John C. *Introduction to Theology.* Scottdale, Pa.: Herald Press, 1954.

156

Scripture quotations taken from the following modern translations:

The New Testament: An American Translation by Edgar J. Goodspeed. The University of Chicago Press. Copyright © 1923, 1948 by the University of Chicago.

The New Testament in Modern English by J. B. Phillips. The Macmillan Company. Copyright © 1958 by J. B. Phillips.

The New Testament of Our Lord and Savior Jesus Christ by John A. Broadus et. al. United Bible Society. American Bible Union Version (ABUV) Improved Edition.

The Paraphrased Epistles by Kenneth N. Taylor. Tyndale House Publishers, Wheaton, Illinois. Copyright © 1962 by Tyndale House Publishers.

The Twentieth Century New Testament. Moody Bible Institute.

INDEX

159

162